797,885 Books

are available to read at

Forgotten Books

www.ForgottenBooks.com

Forgotten Books' App
Available for mobile, tablet & eReader

ISBN 978-1-333-38962-8
PIBN 10498524

This book is a reproduction of an important historical work. Forgotten Books uses state-of-the-art technology to digitally reconstruct the work, preserving the original format whilst repairing imperfections present in the aged copy. In rare cases, an imperfection in the original, such as a blemish or missing page, may be replicated in our edition. We do, however, repair the vast majority of imperfections successfully; any imperfections that remain are intentionally left to preserve the state of such historical works.

Forgotten Books is a registered trademark of FB &c Ltd.
Copyright © 2015 FB &c Ltd.
FB &c Ltd, Dalton House, 60 Windsor Avenue, London, SW19 2RR.
Company number 08720141. Registered in England and Wales.

For support please visit www.forgottenbooks.com

1 MONTH OF FREE READING

at

www.ForgottenBooks.com

By purchasing this book you are eligible for one month membership to ForgottenBooks.com, giving you unlimited access to our entire collection of over 700,000 titles via our web site and mobile apps.

To claim your free month visit: www.forgottenbooks.com/free498524

* Offer is valid for 45 days from date of purchase. Terms and conditions apply.

English
Français
Deutsche
Italiano
Español
Português

www.forgottenbooks.com

Mythology Photography **Fiction** Fishing Christianity **Art** Cooking Essays Buddhism Freemasonry Medicine **Biology** Music **Ancient Egypt** Evolution Carpentry Physics Dance Geology **Mathematics** Fitness Shakespeare **Folklore** Yoga Marketing **Confidence** Immortality Biographies Poetry **Psychology** Witchcraft Electronics Chemistry History **Law** Accounting **Philosophy** Anthropology Alchemy Drama Quantum Mechanics Atheism Sexual Health **Ancient History** **Entrepreneurship** Languages Sport Paleontology Needlework Islam **Metaphysics** Investment Archaeology Parenting Statistics Criminology **Motivational**

JOURNAL OF EDUCATIONAL RESEARCH MONOGRAPHS
B. R. BUCKINGHAM, Editor

No. 3   June, 1922

The Iowa Spelling Scales
Their Derivation, Uses, and Limitations

ERNEST J. ASHBAUGH
Professor of School Administration
and
Assistant Director, Bureau of
Educational Research

OHIO STATE UNIVERSITY

PUBLIC SCHOOL PUBLISHING COMPANY
BLOOMINGTON, ILLINOIS

Copyright 1922
By Public School Publishing Co.
Bloomington, Illinois

ACKNOWLEDGMENTS

This study was undertaken as a direct service to the schools of the State of Iowa through the suggestion of Professor Ernest Horn, to whom I owe the greatest debt of gratitude for continuous encouragement and helpful criticism.

I wish to thank the superintendents, teachers and pupils who gave so freely of their time and effort in securing the spellings and also the Dean of the Graduate College and the Director of the Extension Division who financed from their budgets the collection and scoring of the data.

Acknowledgments are also made to Dean Russell, Associate Professor Lewis, and Dr. Harry A. Greene for their sympathetic counsel and assistance throughout the progress of the study.

E. J. A.

TABLE OF CONTENTS

	PAGE
Section I. Introduction	7-13
Fields of experimental pedagogy	7
Studies in determination of vocabulary	8
Studies in derivation of scales	10
Section II. The Problem	13
Section III. Method of Gathering the Data	14-15
Selection and arrangement of words	14
Cooperation of the schools of the state	14
Section IV. Method of Handling the Data	15-16
Section V. Assumed Distribution of Ability	16-20
Normal probability curve assumed	16
Some properties of the curve	17
Placing words in the scale	18
Section VI. Use of the Scales	20-22
Measurement of status of ability	21
Measurement of growth of ability	22
A minimum spelling list	22
Section VII. Limitation of the Scales	22-26
Number of spellings used	23
Distribution of spellings	24
Words given in list form	24
Words of varying difficulty placed in the same list	25
No zero point on the scale	26
Section VIII. Bibliography	26-27
Section IX. The Iowa Spelling Scale, Grade 2	30-43
Section X. The Iowa Spelling Scale, Grade 3	46-59
Section XI. The Iowa Spelling Scale, Grade 4	62-75
Section XII. The Iowa Spelling Scale, Grade 5	78-91
Section XIII. The Iowa Spelling Scale, Grade 6	94-107
Section XIV. The Iowa Spelling Scale, Grade 7	110-123
Section XV. The Iowa Spelling Scale, Grade 8	123-139
Appendix	142-144
Exhibit A	142
Exhibit B	143
Exhibit C	144

INTRODUCTION

The Iowa Spelling Scales have been extensively used. The relatively large number of words included in them and their freedom from excessive statistical manipulation have rightly commended them to practical workers. They have, however, been out of print for some time. Moreover, even those who are fortunate enough to possess the scales in their original form no doubt realize that they are capable of a more useful presentation.

Accordingly this monograph is offered for those who desire a complete representation of the scale in permanent form. The percents of correct spellings in each grade are given for each of the nearly 3,000 words of the scale. Nowhere else has such a detailed showing of the difficulty of the spelling of words been made.

An account is also given of the derivation of the scale; and this is no inconsiderable contribution. The reader will no doubt be impressed by the author's scientific attitude and by his unwillingness to compromise with his ideals of accuracy through adopting all-too-prevalent devices for smoothing out difficulties and then pretending that such difficulties do not exist.

We are glad to observe the position which Doctor Ashbaugh takes on the question of the degree of difficulty of the words which constitute the best testing material. In substance he says that the nearer they are to 50 percent accuracy for the grade in question the better. There has been a strong tendency among users of spelling tests to select words which were much too easy. This tendency has been fostered partly by the fact that the Ayres Scale lists for each grade only the words spelled by 50 percent or more of the children, and partly by the naive desire to see larger figures. Somehow one thinks more highly of a class average of 87 than of one of 46, although the latter may indicate a better performance.

The publication of the Iowa Spelling Scales in this form will place at the disposal of school people a far larger number of evaluated words than have hitherto been generally available. This richness of material will greatly enhance the usefulness of the scale. Duplicate lists can easily be made, and a prolonged program of testing can be carried on without the necessity of making allowance for practice effects. Moreover, the fact that the words of the scale are selected on the basis of frequency of use in correspondence renders the material particularly appropriate for teaching and drill purposes. In fact as a spelling book this monograph has high value. The appropriateness of the words is assured because of their frequent use in correspondence—that is, in the only situation where spelling ability is sure to be required—while the known difficulty of the words permits intelligent grading and distinctions in teaching emphasis.

B. R. BUCKINGHAM, *Editor.*

SECTION I

INTRODUCTION

Fields of Experimental Pedagogy

The last two decades have witnessed a large amount of work in the field of experimental pedagogy. This has principally followed three general lines, namely, (1) the selection of subject matter, (2) the determination of efficient methods of teaching or learning, and (3) the formulation of more or less objective measures for checking the results.

The Committee on Economy of Time of the National Education Association through its three reports (1) has done a large amount of work in the selection of subject matter. These reports have challenged the attention of superintendents and the recommendations have been written into numerous courses of study. State Teachers' Associations have taken up the work; their committees have attacked the problem and in many cases have added something to this re-direction of education.

The determination of efficient methods of teaching and learning has appealed to psychologists and teachers. In laboratories and experimental schools much time and effort has been spent in gathering bit by bit the evidence for the different subjects. The experimental evidence in reading, writing, spelling, arithmetic, drawing, and music, and such conclusions as are warranted thereby, have been collected from the various schools and are presented by another committee in the Eighteenth Yearbook. (2) Further consideration will not be given to this field since it is not pertinent to the research in this monograph.

The effort in the third line has brought forth the large number of scales and tests now available. The measurement of progress requires an accurate means of measuring initial status. The comparison of one class with another, or of one school system with another, especially when the testing must be done by different persons, also requires a measuring instrument little influenced by different personalities. One of the goals of the makers of standardized tests and scales has been to obtain an objective measuring instrument as little disturbed as possible by the individual using it.

Perhaps in no subject has there been more experimental work done than in spelling. The subject lends itself to careful study in the fields already designated. The investigations which we wish to review briefly as an introduction to the present study have dealt with two problems: (1) the determination of the vocabulary which should be included in children's spelling, and (2) the derivation of objective scales for the measurement of spelling ability.

STUDIES IN THE DETERMINATION OF VOCABULARY

An examination of the tabulation[1] shown in Table I will reveal the fact that the sources investigated for the selection of spelling vocabularies fall into four general groups; (1) occurrence in reading vocabulary, (2) occurrence in school lessons or classroom work, (3) occurrence in children's compositions, and (4) occurrence in correspondence, usually that of adults.

The first attempt to compare carefully the spelling work of different school systems seems to have been reported by Rice (14) in 1897. In 1895 he sent out a list of fifty words to superintend-

TABLE I. CONSPECTUS OF VOCABULARY STUDIES.

AUTHOR	DATE	SOURCE OF MATERIAL
Knowles, Rev. J. (3)	1904	Passages from the Bible and various authors
Eldridge, R. C. (4)	1911	Articles of Sunday Newspapers
Ayres, L. P. (5)	1913	Personal and Business Letters
Jones, W. F. (6)	1913	Children's Composition
Cook, W. A. and O'Shea, M. V. (7)	1914	Family Correspondence
Nicholson, Anne (8) (Editor)	1914	Selected by teachers and supervisors from daily lessons
New Orleans Public School List (9)	1916	Children's School Work
Kansas City Public School List (10)	1916	Selected from pupil's misspelled words and teachers' judgment of words pupils should know how to spell
Houser, J. D. (11)	1916	Letters of farmers
Anderson, W. N. (12)	1917	Written correspondence of Iowa People
Horn, E. (13)	1918	Correspondence of Bankers to Bankers

ents in various sections of the United States. Twenty responded sending in the work of more than 16,000 children. The results of the test showed enormous variations, but a two months' tour spent in visiting the various schools convinced him that much of this variation was due to the peculiar manner in which the examinations had been conducted. Also careful pronunciation of several of the words would have given a clue to the spelling.

---

[1] This tabulation presents only the more important studies from the different sources. For a more complete list see Anderson, W. N. "The determination of a spelling vocabulary based upon written correspondence." (Dissertation, University of Iowa, 1917.)

For these reasons the results of the test were considered unsatisfactory.

A second test involving fifty words in grades four and five, and seventy-five words in grades six, seven, and eight in sentence-dictation form, was given to 13,000 children in eight school systems. In these cases the tests were given under his personal dircetion and checked by his assistants.

Dr. Rice made no statement in his report regarding the manner of selecting his words except that in the second test "special care was exercised to omit words whose pronunciation would tell the secret" (**15**) of the correct spelling.

Too much credit can scarcely be given Rice for his pioneer efforts. He initiated the whole measurement movement. Two criticisms, however, may be directed against his work: (1) the words were not selected on the basis of those which children need to learn to spell; and (2) the words were of greatly varying difficulty but were given equal value in scoring. The best evidence in support of the first point is, that of the 77 words used in the second test, 15 do not occur among the 4,000 words of highest frequency in the combined results of the nine most extensive studies of correspondence.[2] These words are: almanac, ascending, changeable, conscientious, deceive, elegant, fatiguing, hopping, laughter, listened, praise, sensible, slipped, sweeping, whistling. Of these, six do not appear in any form, even the most simple.

Rice recognized that the material for spelling instruction should be selected in such a way as to eliminate unusual words. This is shown by two quotations: "The absurdities incident to the so-called 'natural method' were shown very clearly during one of my visits to a fifth-year class, when the pupils, who had studied the pine, were about to write a composition on the subject. In preparation, the spelling lesson of the day consisted of the following words: exogen, erect, cylindrical, coniferal, irregular, indestructible, pins, resinous, and whorls." (**16**) His fourth recommendation concerning the course in spelling reads thus: "Precedence should be given to common words, while technical and unusual words should be taught incidentally." (**17**) However, he gave us no clue as to how the "common words" should be detected.

That Rice's words were of greatly varying difficulty was pointed out by Thorndike (**18**) who gives the relative frequency of mistakes within the same group of children for each of the forty-nine words taken by Dr. Rice to be equal measures of spell-

---

[2] The results of this compilation have not been published. Access to the data was secured through the kindness of Dr. Horn.

ing ability. These forty-nine range from a frequency of forty-two errors to zero. Unfortunately, the table does not give the total number of children attempting the test, so it cannot be placed on a percentage basis.

The reader's attention is called to Table II. This table gives the frequency of error of fifth-grade children on five of Dr. Rice's words as found by Thorndike and the percent of error of fifth-grade children on the same words as shown by the Ayres scale and the present study.

TABLE II. DIFFERENCE IN DIFFICULTY OF FIVE WORDS REGARDED BY DR. RICE AS OF EQUAL DIFFICULTY.

Word	Frequency of Error Grade V—Thorndike	Percentage of Error Grade V—Ayres	Percentage of Error Grade V—Ashbaugh
necessary	42	58	77
disappoint	37	79	64
learn	3	12	14
because	1	6	6
picture	0	8	5

STUDIES IN DERIVATION OF SCALES

The studies intended to evaluate the words to be used in measuring spelling ability have been but two in number previous to this monograph.

Buckingham. (**19**) In 1913, Buckingham presented the educational world with the first spelling scale. He did preliminary testing with a list of 270 words selected from a much larger list of graded words used by the author in his own school. These had been selected by taking from five of the popular spelling books then in use, a vocabulary of 5,000 words agreed upon by two or more of the books, and then following two principles: (1) "that all of them should be sufficiently common to be in the speaking vocabulary of third-grade children," and (2) "that the spelling difficulty of many of them should be great enough to test the ability of eighth-grade children." (**20**)

These words were placed in sentences and dictated to grades three to eight. On the basis of the results, a group of 100 words were chosen which in general showed the following characteristics: (1) That the word was not so difficult that it offered no test of third-grade ability. (2) That it showed a steady increase through the following grades but did not reach so high a figure in the highest grades as to prevent its being a test of ability there.

These words were placed in sentences and their difficulty determined by additional testing. By this process he finally arrived at a first and a second preferred list of 25 words each. In order to get a measure of zero ability, an easy list of fifty words was devised. These words were then evaluated with a high degree of precision and were presented for testing purposes in the form of ten-, twenty-five-, and fifty-word scales.

The small number of words limits the usefulness of the scale since the entire list can be quickly learned to 100 percent median accuracy by a class of ordinary ability in the upper grades. The study is of great interest to advanced students of education because of the great refinement of method. It is doubtful, however, if the high degree of refinement adds anything to the value of the scale for practical use by teachers, principals, and superintendents in the field.

Ayres. (21) Probably the most advanced step in spelling measurement was taken by Ayres in 1915 in presenting his Measuring Scale for Ability in Spelling. The 1,000 words in this scale were secured by combining "the results of the several studies so as to secure the most reliable list as a foundation for the work." (22) The placing of the "one thousand commonest words" in the measuring scale assumes that children should be taught and be able to spell these "commonest words" even though they are unable to spell other words. With this assumption we agree.

Two criticisms will be offered concerning the selection of the words:

1. The list is a hybrid since it is made up by combining correspondence frequencies with newspaper and literary frequencies. A comparison of these 1,000 words with the most extensive studies of correspondence reveals 33 words which never occur in these correspondence lists, and 71 others which do not occur in the 3,000 words of greatest frequency. Such words as: arrest, convict, capture, estate, jail, mayor, police, testimony, victim, and witness, occur frequently in newspapers but only a few people ever have any occasion to write them. Why then should they be admitted to our minimal spelling lists?

2. In the selection of these words, root forms and derivatives were counted as one form unless they presented "different spelling difficulties." "Plurals and verb forms presenting no characteristic spelling difficulties beyond those inherent in the singular or infinitive have not been included. (23) Researches by the writer (24) have convinced him that almost without exception derived forms are spelled with less accuracy than root forms, however simple the change involved, and that one cannot select by inspection the forms having slight variation from those having wide variation.

A further criticism must be made on the regularity of the advancement of words in the scale. If all words were learned at the same rate, this regularity might exist. Buckingham found that most of the words which he tried out did not progress regularly and that frequently there was a reversal instead of advance in accuracy from one grade to another.

He says, "In order that this list should be of greatest value it should be so constituted that the increases in percents correct so keep pace with the increase from grade to grade of general spelling ability that a word tends in all grades to maintain the same difficulty relative to all other words in the list to which it belongs. A word which is twentieth in point of difficulty for the third grade ought to deviate as little as possible from the same rank in the other grades. The experience gained in making this investigation leads us to think that most words do not meet this condition, even approximately. The span between the third and the eighth grades is very wide. Accordingly, a very large class of words is impossible for the earlier yet easy for the later grades. Still others are really difficult in the lower grades, but of almost no difficulty in the upper grades." (25)

The following illustration from Buckingham's Preferred Lists show that although he purposely rejected the most irregular words, irregularities still existed.

TABLE III. PERCENT OF ACCURACY WITH WHICH CHILDREN OF SUCCESSIVE GRADES SPELLED EACH OF THE GIVEN WORDS.[3]

Word	Third	Fourth	Fifth	Sixth	Seventh	Eighth
saucer	11	29	42	58	79	81
raise	21	54	67	84	93	94
already	16	42	43	62	44	77
grease	11	18	37	35	42	57

This table is read as follows: The word "saucer" was spelled by third-grade children with an average accuracy of 11 percent; by fourth-grade children with 29 percent; by fifth-grade children with 42 percent, etc. The percents for the other words in the different grades are read in the same manner.

The first two words show rather consistent increases up to the seventh grade and practically no increase from seventh to eighth. The other two show actual instances of lower accuracy of spelling in one grade than in the previous grade.

The present study shows numerous illustrations of the same phenomenon. Since no word was rejected, lapses appeared, as might have been anticipated from the fact that they occurred in Buckingham's highly selected list. Further, these lapses occur

---

[3] These words with their accuracies were selected from Buckingham, B. R. *Spelling Ability—Its Measurement and Distribution.* Table III, page 14.

much more frequently in cases of high accuracy (i. e., very easy words) than in those of medium or low.

Because of these findings, a serious question must be raised concerning the amount of smoothing which Ayres must have done to get the perfect regularity from grade to grade which he has upon his scale.

In order to present the situation as it was actually found, it was decided to provide in the present study a separate scale for each of the grades and to include in each scale the whole number of words. Ayres arbitrarily rejected from consideration all words for each grade whose accuracy fell below the middle step. In the present study, no smoothing has been done to show regularity of progress from grade to grade and no words have been rejected from any grade scale regardless of the low percent of accuracy involved.

In the field of measurement, the Ayres scale has had a much wider influence than that by Buckingham. More than eighty-five thousand copies have been distributed in less than four years. Many spelling tests, such as those by Courtis (26), Monroe (27), Fordyce (28), and the writer (29) have been based directly upon it, and probably hundreds of superintendents have adopted it outright as a minimal list for their schools.

SECTION II

THE PROBLEM

Extension work by the writer among the school people of Iowa has brought the following facts clearly to his attention:

1. School people are eager to use the results of scientific research in their school rooms.
2. They have used and appreciated the Ayres Spelling Scale but rightly think that there should be a larger list.
3. For this larger list to be of most worth, the words must be evaluated in some manner.

It was therefore believed that a distinct service would be rendered the schools of the state if a much larger list, scientifically selected, should be evaluated and made available.

At the time the work was begun, the most extensive study of correspondence vocabulary was that of W. N. Anderson. Through the tabulation of 3723 letters of Iowa people, 361,184 running words revealed 3105 different words having such a frequency as to justify, in his judgment, their being taught in school. The Anderson list was an Iowa correspondence list, scientifically selected and containing sufficient words for a much larger list than had ever before been evaluated. Thus the problem became definite—*the making of an Iowa Spelling Scale.*

SECTION III

METHOD OF GATHERING THE DATA

Selection and Arrangement of Words

For administrative convenience, only 3,000 words were taken from Anderson's list. The words were listed in order of decreasing frequency and the first 3,000 were arbitrarily chosen. These 3,000 were divided into three sets of 1,000 words each, dividing the frequency as equally as possible. For example, the words *and*, *the* and *to* being in order the words of greatest frequency in Anderson's tabulation, became the first word respectively of each of the three sets. The 4th, 5th and 6th words in order of highest frequency became respectively the second words of each set, and so on. Each set of 1,000 was then divided into ten lists of 100 words each.[4] In each set, the 1st, 11th, 21st, etc. words became list 1; the 2nd, 12th, 22nd, etc. became list 2; etc. Thus each list included words ranging from very high to lowest frequency of occurrence in Anderson's study. These lists were printed 100 words on a sheet, and the ten lists of a set clipped together.

Co-operation of the Schools of the State

An invitation to co-operate in a state-wide survey of spelling was sent to the superintendents of schools in all cities and towns of the state, having a population of 1,000 or more. A few smaller places were also invited to participate. More than 150 superintendents promised the co-operation of their teachers in this work. Enough sets of words were sent to each of these superintendents to supply his teachers and printed instructions accompanied each set. A copy of these instructions and list 1 of the set will be found on pages 142 and 143.

These instructions requested ten days work from each class. The children in Grades II-IV were to spell 500 words at the rate of 50 per day and those in Grades V-VIII were to spell 1,000 words at the rate of 100 per day. All spellings were to be made without preliminary study or any teacher help. Children in all grades were thus asked to spell all the different words, although it was surmised that many of them would not be spelled by lower grade children. Preliminary experiments, however, had definitely shown that one could not predict with a high degree of accuracy what words the pupils in any particular grade would misspell.[5]

---

[4] The reason for the division of the 3,000 words into sets of 1,000 and lists of 100 will be understood from the instructions to teachers. See page 143.

[5] A very simple experiment in this line was made by the writer with his University class composed of school superintendents and teachers. List 1 of the present study (see page 142) was given to each member of the class with

It was therefore deemed necessary to ask a large number of pupils in each grade (II-VIII inclusive) to attempt to spell each word.

After the 3,000 words were printed and sent out, it was discovered that there were twenty-three words duplicated. Seventeen of these were duplicated in Anderson's original list, while there were six other duplicates due to typographical errors. Thus the list of 3,000 was reduced to 2,977, the number which appears in the completed scales.

The response of the superintendents, teachers and pupils was most gratifying. More than 100 school systems were able to do the work and send in the results. A list of these cities and towns is given on page 144. A conservative estimate indicates that nearly 1,400 teachers and 45,000 children participated in the work

SECTION IV

METHOD OF HANDLING THE DATA

This very generous response brought in several times as much material as could be used. Hence, a random selection of papers on each list was made from all schools returning data in any grade. This means that on the average, about thirty-five cities and towns are represented by pupils in the determination of the position of each word in each scale. At least 200 spellings were used for each word and the total number of spellings used on the 2977 words in the seven grades was 4,662,200.

All data used were scored or re-checked by the writer or by assistants carefully instructed by him. As has been found by everyone investigating spelling, a number of arbitrary decisions had to be made. Words omitted; words illegibly written; words

---

the request that he should mark each word as follows: H if in his judgment the pupils of fifth grade would spell the word with an accuracy of from 67 percent to 100 percent; M if they would spell with an accuracy of 34 percent to 66 percent; and L if they would spell with an accuracy of 33 percent or less. The results showed that in spite of the great latitude allowed, but 45 percent of the judgments were correct as compared with the results in this monograph; 31 percent of the judgments were one unit wrong and 14 percent were two units wrong. Two units wrong means that words which pupils spelled with an accuracy of 67 percent or higher were judged as 33 percent or lower and vice versa. Even when the nineteen words whose spelling accuracies by the pupils fell within 5 percent of the dividing points, 33-34 and 66-67, were not considered, only 48 percent of the judgments were correct; 40 percent were wrong one unit and 12 percent were wrong two units. In other words, when experienced school men and women attempted to judge the accuracy with which children would spell a set of words, they were more than 10 percent wrong with more than half the cases and more than 33 percent wrong in 12 to 14 percent of the cases.

substituted due to misunderstanding the pronunciation; wrong form of homonyms; changes in number and tense except when the change involved an addition to, but no change in, the form given were all counted wrong. But one form of spelling for a word was considered right except the few words for which Webster's New International Dictionary lists two spellings as equally correct.

SECTION V

ASSUMED DISTRIBUTION OF ABILITY

It was stated in Section II that part of the problem was the evaluation of the words which had been scientifically selected. When the percent of accuracy of spelling has been determined, one form of evaluation has been made, but this is not entirely satisfactory, as will be shown later.

NORMAL PROBABILITY CURVE ASSUMED

Figure 1 presents a typical normal probability or normal frequeney curve. The curve has the mass of its area in the central part and but a small part near the ends.

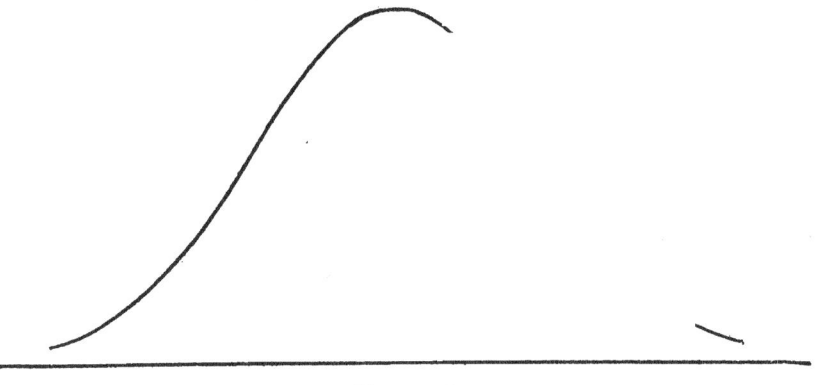

FIGURE 1

This form of distribution has been found to hold true in such human traits as height, weight, length of arms, etc. The great majority of adult men cluster closely around the mean height or weight of all adult men while a decreasing number divide about equally in varying above and below this mean. Only a few vary widely, but those who do are about equally divided as to the direction of their variation.

Does this normal frequency distribution hold true in mental as well as physical traits?

It is a well recognized fact that people with mediocre ability are much more numerous than the dull or the brilliant, and that the very dull and very brilliant are few indeed. Hence, common observation would suggest that general mental ability is distributed in the same manner as physical traits. Does this hold true, also, of the distribution of special abilities such as spelling, arithmetic, language, etc?

The various scales for measuring special abilities such as the Buckingham and Ayres Spelling, Woody's Arithmetic (**30**), Green's Organization (**31**), and Trabue's Language (**32**), have been developed upon the assumption that special abilities are so distributed. The best proof perhaps that the assumption is valid, is that if the assumption is made the results that follow are in very close agreement with the known facts. For these reasons, it was decided to make the same assumption in the present study.

SOME PROPERTIES OF THE CURVE

The mathematical properties of the normal probability curve have been very carefully and elaborately worked out on two bases, namely, the Probable Error (P. E.) or mean deviation, and the Sigma (σ) or standard deviation.

The Probable Error, as a function of the normal probability curve, is that perpendicular distance from the mean at which, if an ordinate is erected, the surface included between this ordinate, the curve, the mean ordinate, and the base line includes 25 percent of the surface included by the whole curve and the base line.[6] In

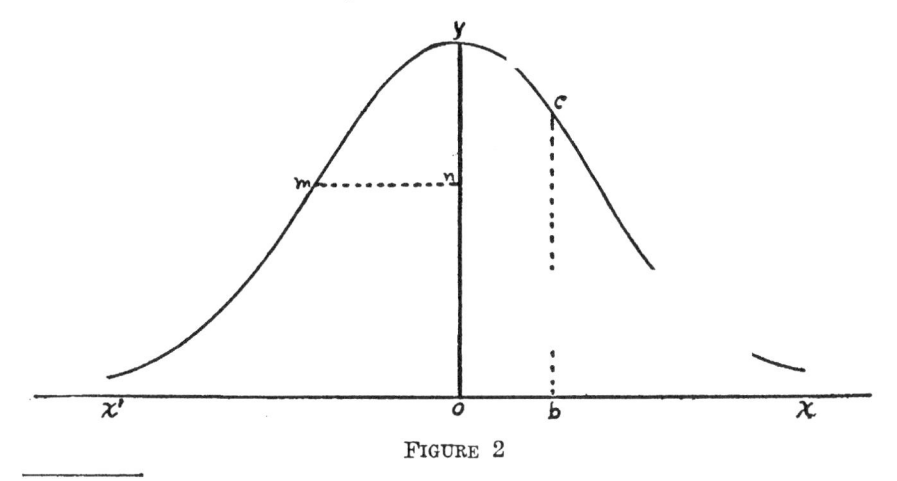

FIGURE 2

---

[6] In theory the curve and base never meet, the lines being in asymptote, but for practical purposes they are considered as meeting at some given distance from the mean. It is in this sense that we may speak of the surface included between the curve and the base.

Figure 2, *ob* is 1 P. E. distance and *bcyo* includes 25 percent of the surface $x\ y\ x'$.

Likewise, Sigma or the standard deviation, as a function of the normal probability curve, is the perpendicular distance to the mean ordinate from the point on the curve where it changes from concave to convex; *mn* in Figure 2 represents this distance.

Both Probable Error and Sigma, being functions of the normal probability curve, bear constant relationship to the curve regardless of the variability of base and altitude. Through easily accessible tables, the amount of area included by the curve, mean, base, and an ordinate erected at any given Probable Error or Sigma distance, can be found.[7]

Buckingham, in the development of his spelling scale, used Probable Error and arbitrarily broke off the curve (which theoretically forever approaches the base but never meets it) at ± 4.6 P. E. This disregards but about one-tenth of one percent of the total surface on either side of the mean.

Ayres, in making his scale, used Sigma and arbitrarily broke the extremities at ± 2.5 σ which disregards about six-tenths of one percent at each end.

After considerable experimentation, the writer decided to follow Ayres and use the ± 2.5 σ curve for the following reasons:

1. In practical schoolroom work it is doubtful if it is worth while to differentiate spelling differences of less than one percent. To extend the curve beyond ± 2.5 σ which is approximately the same as ± 3.75 P. E., necessitates this finer differentiation.

2. Since 893 words[8] are common to the Ayres Scale and this study, the use of the same form of distribution would permit comparisons not possible otherwise.

Placing Words in the Scale·

Having assumed the normal probability curve, and having decided upon the measure of variability to use and the limits at which the curve should be arbitrarily broken off, the next problem was to decide on the number of steps into which to divide the base. The spelling accuracies varied in most grades from at or near zero on some words to at or near 100 percent on others. That is, there were some words which children of any grade spelled with perfect or nearly perfect accuracy while there were other words which were missed by all or nearly all the children.

---

[7] For further discussion of the theory of the normal probability curve, the reader is referred to: Rugg, H. O., *Statistical Method Applied to Education*, Ch. VII.

[8] There are 893 words which appear in both studies which are identical in form while there are 25 others which differ in suffix only. Of these, 10 differ in the suffix "e-d" and 5 in the suffix "s."

In theory the number of steps or divisions into which the base may be divided is infinite, but practical considerations limit the number to but a few. Since our assumption of normal distribution predicates that the number of very good and very poor spellers are few, it is necessary to make finer discriminations between those percentages lying near the extremes of the scale than between those lying near the middle. The larger the number of steps or divisions into which the base is divided, the finer the distinctions drawn all along the scale, but especially is this true near the extremes. As has been stated, however, a finer discrimination than whole percentages can hardly be justified in an instrument designed for practical schoolroom measurement. On the other hand, but few divisions would tend to cover up differences which should be revealed.

Again, after much experimentation it was decided that the division of the base line into twenty-five equal steps, as Ayres did, gave the best results since it permits single whole percentage discrimination of differences near the extremes and does not group together too large percentage differences in the middle.

If there were an equal number of each grade of ability, excellent, good, fair, poor, and very poor; that is, if the frequency surface were a rectangle, then the percentage valuation would be very satisfactory. But we know this is not true and have assumed the distribution to be that of the probability curve instead. Therefore, words which differ by a single percent in the accuracy of spelling do not always represent equal differences in difficulty. Reference to Figure 1 will show quickly that the linear distance between two ordinates so erected as to include between them, the base and the curve, one percent of the whole surface will differ much depending upon whether the ordinates are erected near the median or near the extremes. One of these twenty-five parts into which we have divided the base will underlie approximately nine percent of the surface if located at the median, about four percent if located midway between the median and the extremes and only one percent if located near the extremes. It is this recognition of the type of distribution of ability which makes the percentage evaluation unsatisfactory.

On the basis of the accuracy of the children's spellings, each word was then placed in its proper step or position on the scale. Because it was thought that students of experimental education might care to have the finer distinctions which are not afforded by the step position alone, it was decided to keep the percentage groups within the steps of the scale separate and designate the exact percentage accuracy with which each word was spelled by the children.

If the difficulty of words be defined in terms of differences in position among the steps of the scale, then the words which lie in a single step are of approximately equal difficulty and the words in one step are as much more difficult than those in the previous step as the words in any other step are more difficult than those in the step preceding it. That is, the degree of difficulty between steps is constant throughout the length of the scale.

It will be perceived, of course, that the difficulty of spelling a word is thus defined in terms of the accuracy with which children in a given grade responded to the word under the conditions described in this monograph. It has nothing to do with the inherent difficulties of teaching or learning the word except to the extent that these may be reflected in the accuracy of the spellings of the pupils.

Throughout this monograph, spelling ability is spoken of in terms of efficiency of performance. The only measure of ability which we have for mental traits is in terms of performance. This is common usage and we believe it is perfectly justifiable. We measure ability to read, ability to add, ability to hit a target, ability to lift a weight, etc., in terms of performance. In all these activities, we find by measuring a large number of cases that a few are very good, a few very poor and the majority of all cases occupy an intermediate position. In other words, these various abilities distribute themselves about in the form of the normal probability surface of frequency. It has been the assumption upon which these scales have been built, that spelling ability, ability to do this particular thing under the given conditions, is distributed in this same manner. The scales do not concern themselves with the child's inherent capacity to learn to do, or the difficulties inherent in the words themselves.

SECTION VI

USE OF THE SCALES

These scales lend themselves to at least three uses, namely, (1) measurement of status of spelling ability, (2) measurement of growth in spelling ability, and (3) a minimal spelling list for teaching purposes.

Each word having been placed in the scales on the basis of the accuracy with which children in the respective grade spelled it when presented in ordinary list form, any teacher, principal, or superintendent may use the scale to determine how well his own class or school can spell any group of these words in comparison with the children of Iowa as a whole. In making this comparison, the following things should be remembered.

1. That to secure comparable results, the words should be pronounced in accordance with the original instructions (See page 143) and the words scored according to the criteria stated on page 15.

2. That these spellings were from pupils who had on the average completed approximately one-half of the year's work for the grade. Tests given at the beginning or end of the year's work should be interpreted accordingly.

3. That to secure equally reliable results, a much larger list of words must be used with a small group of pupils than with a large group.

4. That in general, words located near the middle of the scale, those with an accuracy of 35 percent-65 percent, are probably more reliable for measuring purposes than those near the extremes.

Words spelled with 100 percent accuracy furnish no test because all the children have mastered them. Some of them could undoubtedly spell much more difficult words. Likewise, words which are missed by all the children furnish no test since we have no means of knowing how much too difficult they are. Since there are many possibilities of wrong spelling against one possible right form, it is probable that 50 percent represents the maximum point of critical measure of a group. This conforms with the experimental work of Otis. (33)

Measurement of Status of Ability

In using the scales for measuring class and school status, it should be kept in mind that words of differing percents within a step are of approximately equal difficulty but to equalize even small differences, a random selection of words from all the percentage groups in a step should be made and these words pronounced as an ordinary spelling test without instruction or previous study. If the average of the class is the same as the average for the step or within the limits of the percents listed under one step, the class has a spelling status on these words about the same as the children of like grade in Iowa. If the class average reaches a percent higher than the highest listed under the step, the class is above average; if below the lowest listed under the step, it is below average.

A word of caution is perhaps in place. The teacher in using these scales must remember that the fundamental assumption upon which the scales have been built is that spelling ability distributes itself according to the normal probability surface of frequency. It must not be expected, therefore, that all the children in her class will spell all the words in a given test, even though the words are chosen from a single step on the scale, with the same percent of accuracy. A wide range of variation is to be expected and a very narrow range would be quite unusual. Further, the words in a step have been placed there as of approximate equality on the basis of a large number of spellings and it is not to be expected that, with a small group such as a class, the accuracy of spelling on each of the words will be equal.

MEASUREMENT OF GROWTH OF ABILITY

In measurement of growth, two objects may be distinguished, (1) the measurement of growth or change due to a term or year of school work, and (2) the measurement of growth or change due to the use of a special method, device, or time variation during a greater or less period.

The first measurement will probably be the one of most significance to teachers and superintendents, and gross differences will be of greatest interest. For this reason, the differences may well be considered mainly in terms of step changes.

The second measurement will be of primary interest to special supervisors and students of experimental education. Since these persons are interested in more refined results, they should consider the individual percentage groups within the step. Whole step differences may frequently be larger than the changes brought about by the conditions involved in the experiment.

A MINIMAL SPELLING LIST

This list presents with a high degree of accuracy the words which people use most frequently in written correspondence. For this reason it is highly important that pupils in the elementary school learn to spell these words. By using the words of the scale as the material for regular class instruction, teachers may note class improvement, but they must recognize that as a scale it is becoming less and less valuable as a measuring instrument. However, the writer agrees completely with Ayres when he says, "Probably the scale will have served its greatest usefulness in any locality when the school children have mastered these words so thoroughly that the scale has become quite useless as a measuring instrument." (**34**)

SECTION VII

LIMITATIONS OF THE SCALES

The scales presented herewith are subject to certain limitations, some of which will be discussed in this section.

Number of Spellings Used

In general, with a random selection the reliability of results increases as the square root of the number of cases involved. In the following scales, the number of spellings on each word in each grade was 200 or more. This number was selected as being a sufficient number to give a degree of reliability acceptable in this type of measurement.

However, in order to ascertain the range of variability which might be expected on the basis of 200 spellings in comparison with a larger number, 700 spellings were selected at random on a list of 100 words. The accuracy of spelling on each word was checked out per 100 spellings and three combinations of 200 each were compared with the accuracy of 700. The spelling accuracy of the 100 words in the 700 spellings varied from 100 percent for the three easiest words to 11, 15 and 20 percent respectively on the three most difficult words.

Since the words were to be placed in the scales in terms of steps of equal value as stated previously, it was thought that this examination of reliability of placement should be in terms of steps rather than in terms of percent. The total scale was divided arbitrarily into three-step groups on each side of the middle step. Then the three on each side adjacent to the middle step and this middle step were thrown together since there seemed no valid reason for keeping them separate, the percents in each step being symmetrically placed above and below the middle step. When the 100 words were distributed according to this grouping on the basis of accuracies obtained from the 700 spellings of each word, it was found that there were 12 words in the easiest group, 32 in the next, and so on as shown in column four of Table II.

Next the accuracy for each word on the basis of each of the first, second, and third 200 spellings was taken from its accuracy

TABLE IV. AVERAGE DEVIATION OF SPELLING ACCURACY IN TERMS OF SCALE STEP OF RANDOM SAMPLINGS OF 200 SPELLINGS FROM THE ACCURACIES OF 700 SPELLINGS.

Accuracy in Percents on 700 Spellings	Number of Scale Steps Within These Limits	Average Range in Percent Included in One Step	Number of Words in Group	Average Deviation in Scale Step First 200	Second 200	Third 200
98-100	3	1.00	12	.42	.42	.42
91-97	3	2.33	32	.55	.60	.63
77-90	3	4.67	20	.49	.69	.41
24-76	7	7.57	33	.38	.27	.34
10-23	3	4.67	3	.50	.07	.93

on the basis of the total 700 and the average difference of deviation of all words within the group was determined. This average deviation in terms of percent was then converted into average deviation in terms of scale step by dividing by the average range in percent included in one step.

From these data it is concluded that since the average variation is less than 0.7 of a step in all cases but one, and is 0.5 of a step or less in more than half the cases, 200 spellings is amply sufficient for the degree of accuracy required in placing the words in a scale of this type.

Distribution of Spellings

It may be considered a limitation on the scales that all spellings used were secured from Iowa school children. The answer to this is two-fold: (1) that the scales were designed primarily for service to the school people of the state of Iowa. From this standpoint this limitation becomes a positive recommendation. (2) On the basis of a state-wide study of spelling, involving 8818 children in Grades III to VIII inclusive, on spelling tests devised from the Ayres scale, the school children of Iowa spell with about the same average accuracy as children in the 86 cities involved in the Ayres study. This is shown by Table V.

TABLE V. COMPARATIVE SPELLING RESULTS: AYRES SCALE AND 27 IOWA CITIES. 20 WORDS, LIST SPELLING.

Grades	Third	Fourth	Fifth	Sixth	Seventh	Eighth
Number of Children	1620	1635	1841	1338	1228	1156
Iowa Average Scores	73	85	74	83	77	86
Ayres Standard	73	88	73	84	73	84

The table is read as follows: 1620 third-grade children spelled the 20 words with an average accuracy of 73 percent and the Ayres standard for these words is also 73 percent; 1635 fourth-grade Iowa children spelled the 20 words with an average accuracy of 85 percent while the Ayres standard on these words is 88 percent. The number of children and the average accuracy for Iowa children and the Ayres standard for the other grades are read in the same manner.

Words Given in List Form

It is recognized that the spelling of words in list form does not give an exact measure of the accuracy with which children will spell words in their ordinary daily work. This condition is perhaps more closely approximated by a timed-dictation test. In neither case, however, can we be certain that the ability displayed is exactly the same as that which will function when the child is writing spontaneously. These scales do present the accuracy with which children did spell these words when presented under the conditions described in the monograph.

WORDS OF VARYING DIFFICULTY PRESENTED IN THE SAME LIST

Making up the list of words on the basis of approximately equal distribution of words of high, median, and low frequency in written correspondence necessarily brought into the same list, words of widely varying difficulty. How far this tends to produce an inaccurate result in the spelling of the common words is not definitely known.

Due to the fact that 23 words were duplicated in the lists sent out, it is possible to make some comparison between the accuracy with which words were spelled when they occurred early in the list, preceded by words which were comparatively easy, and when the same words occurred late in the list, preceded by words of greater difficulty. Thirteen of these 23 words involved this situation of appearing one time rather early in the list and a second time rather late. A comparison of the accuracy with which the children in each of the different grades spelled the word when it occurred early in the list with the accuracy with which it was spelled by children of the same grade when it occurred late in the list, showed two things:

1. That in all grades there was a somewhat higher average accuracy on the words when they occurred early in the list, though some words showed the opposite situation. The median increase in accuracy in the seven grades on words occurring early in the list over the accuracy on the same words when occurring late in the list was but 2 percent. This difference in accuracy was greatest in the third and fourth grades, though a priori judgment had decided that this factor would most affect second-grade children and have less influence thereafter from grade to grade.

2. The average difference of spelling accuracy in these two grades which seemed to be most greatly influenced by this factor was practically identical with the range of percents included in a single step in the portion of the scale in which these words appear.

Since these words were placed in the scales in an intermediate position determined by the average accuracy of spelling in the two positions, it is quite certain that no word is misplaced more than a single step. It is probable that half the words are misplaced less than half a step (that is, not at all in the scale) due to this factor.

No Zero Point on the Scale

These scales in common with the Ayres scale, place the words on the basis of relative difficulty rather than absolute difficulty from a point which would indicate no ability at all. Because of this limitation, it is not possible to state that words appearing in any single step are so many "times as" difficult as words appearing in some other step. It is only possible to state that words in any step are as much more difficult than the words in the step preceding as the words in any other step are more difficult than the words in the step preceding that. In other words, the inter-step difficulty is approximately equal throughout the scale.

From the standpoint of practical usage the lack of an absolute zero-point presents no serious objection. In the measurement of progress, school people are interested in making comparison with norms and with previous status rather than in determining "times as" relationships. For this reason, a zero-point was not considered of sufficient importance to justify the large amount of additional work which would have been necessary to have secured it.

SECTION VIII

BIBLIOGRAPHY

1. *Fourteenth, Sixteenth and Seventeenth Yearbooks of the National Society for the Study of Education*, 1915, 1917 and 1918.
2. *Eighteenth Yearbook of the National Society for the Study of Education.* Pt. II, 1919.
3. Knowles, Rev. J. *The London Point System of Reading for the Blind.* London, 1904.
4. Eldridge, R. C. *Six Thousand Common English Words*, Niagara Falls, New York, 1911.
5. Ayres, L. P. *The Spelling Vocabularies of Personal and Business Letters.* Russell Sage Foundation, 1913.
6. Jones, W. F. *Concrete Investigation of the Material of English Spelling.* University of South Dakota, Vermilion, South Dakota, 1913.
7. Cook, W. A. and O'Shea, M. V. *The Child and His Spelling.* Bobbs-Merrill Company, 1914.
8. Nicholson, Anne (Editor.) *A Speller for the Use of the Teachers of California.* Sacramento, California, 1914.
9. *New Orleans Public School List.* School Bulletin, 1916.
10. *Bureau of Educational Research Bulletin No. 2.* Kansas City, Missouri, 1916.
11. Houser, J. D. An Investigation of the Writing Vocabularies of Representatives of an Economic Class. *Elementary School Journal.* 17:70 8-18.

12. Anderson, W. N. *The Determination of a Spelling Vocabulary Based Upon Written Correspondence.* Dissertation, University of Iowa, 1917.
13. Horn, E. *A Study of the Vocabulary of Letters Written by Bankers to Bankers About Banking.* (Unpublished.)
14. Rice, J. M. Futility of the Spelling Grind. *Forum* 23:163-72, 1897. Later published again in *Scientific Management in Education,* New York, 1913.
15. Rice, J. M. *Scientific Management in Education.* p. 71.
16. Ibid. p. 93.
17. Ibid. p. 94.
18. Thorndike, E. L. *Mental and Social Measurements.* p. 8.
19. Buckingham, B. R. *Spelling Ability, Its Measurement and Distribution.* Columbia Contributions to Education No. 59, 1913.
20. Ibid. p. 6.
21. Ayres, L. P. *Measurement of Ability in Spelling.* Russell Sage Foundation, 1915.
22. Ibid. p. 8.
23. Ibid. p. 11.
24. Ashbaugh, E. J. and Horn, E. Necessity of Teaching Derived Forms in Spelling. *Journal of Educational Psychology,* 10:143-52, March, 1919. Also Variation in the Spelling of Root and Derived Forms of Words. (Unpublished.)
25. Buckingham, B. R. Op. cit. p. 13.
26. Courtis, S. A. *Standard Research Tests in Spelling.* Detroit 1916.
27. Monroe, W. S. *Timed Sentence Spelling Tests.* Emporia, Kansas, 1916.
28. Fordyce, Charles. *The Nebraska Spelling Test.* University of Nebraska.
29. Ashbaugh, E. J. *Iowa Dictation Exercise and Spelling Tests.* University of Iowa, 1916.
30. Woody, C. *Measurement of Some Achievements in Arithmetic.* Columbia Contributions to Education No. 80, 1916.
31. Greene, H. A. *Tests for the Measurement of Linguistic Organization in Sentences.* Dissertation, University of Iowa, 1919.
32. Trabue, M. R. *Completion-Test Language Scales.* Columbia Contribution to Education No. 77, 1916.
33. Otis, A. S. Reliability of Spelling Scales. *School and Society,* 4:676-83, 716-22, 750-56, 793-96, October 28, November 4, 11, 18, 1916.
34. Ayres, L. P. Op. cit. p. 41.

SECTION IX

THE IOWA SPELLING SCALE

GRADE II

GRADE II

STEP 5—94%
    95%
day
it
    94%
and
is
me

STEP 6—92%
    93%
he
to-day
    92%
are
at
    91%
can

STEP 7—88%
    90%
all
the
you
    89%
be
go
    88%
dog
not
see
she
    87%
boy
may
my
was

STEP 8—84%
    86%
good
    85%
book
for
if
    84%
little
    83%
come
do
his
how

in
let
that
    82%
did
look
so
tell

STEP 9—79%
    81%
have
no
up
will
    80%
big
but
land
old
say
ten
    79%
ago
an
hand
hen
into
of
on
us
    78%
as
last
man
to
tree
your
    77%
away
cat
fat
gold
out
run
way
we

STEP 10—73%
    76%
cow
dear

get
play
some
told
    75%
ball
cannot
hat
ring
this
    74%
them
wind
    73%
cold
door
girl
lot
or
think
    72%
bee
doing
got
May
sat
three
toy
    71%
baby
eat
has
home
pie
seeing
then
    70%
bad
dad
looking
much
thing
time
year

STEP 11—66%
    69%
bell
cap
corn
five
hit
love
over

singing
they
with
    68%
age
am
box
came
going
hill
its
like
mad
pig
playing
red
ship
thank
top
    67%
call
end
far
from
give
had
stop
    66%
free
ice
king
pin
put
    65%
bed
being
by
fast
feet
fill
find
flat
green
lay
made
Miss
night
one
sun
    64%
bat
glad
grass
her

The Iowa Spelling Scales

inside	lost	cake	*52%*
make	papa	coat	about
milk	pen	holding	art
most	poor	left	ate
must	rich	morning	cool
net	room	nut	fell
same	seen	plan	life
telling	snow	rose	low
63%	sold	shop	near
hot	soon	slip	pass
name	sport	stove	place
now	take		rug
wall	took		saying
	west	STEP 13—50%	sell
STEP 12—58%	what		spell
	58%	*54%*	spot
62%	aside	ask	within
apple	asleep	bear	*51%*
band	fun	beside	around
bill	him	blow	city
each	landing	born	forget
fall	miss	dust	hall
nine	mother	farm	just
when	pay	feed	kind
yet	sin	finding	list
61%	state	helping	pick
bid	tip	lake	stay
cup	*57%*	late	Sunday
down	can't	long	town
ever	cut	post	upon
kiss	fish	price	wife
mill	food	ride	*50%*
part	grade	seed	been
rest	hay	song	bit
school	here	too	black
send	met	well	blank
six	rain	*53%*	brand
tent	sleep	along	car
till	wet	bank	fee
want	*56%*	belong	gather
60%	child	date	grand
bay	game	deep	head
cent	keep	foot	hers
forgot	lift	happy	print
gave	mud	joy	shall
hold	rock	kill	side
live	sit	noon	silk
Mr.	small	plow	sis
sent	tenth	sad	spring
stand	than	said	tie
standing	there	set	very
week	trip	shot	went
wish	win	snowing	*49%*
59%	yes	two	arm
best	*55%*	under	display
bring	after	war	faster
income	back	where	finger

The Iowa Spelling Scales

gate
Jan.
mind
nap
never
our
read
rod
roll
soft
spent
step
street
such
wanting

48%

bake
begin
drop
feeding
four
gray
hard
inch
letter
note
paper
pine
raining
rate
real
sheep
starting
thanking
wide
wool
work

47%

able
cord
fine
form
glass
goldfish
light
mamma
meat
nor
oh
order
plate
sight
sister
sweet
thin
were

while
why

46%

barn
became
become
blue
bog
coming
fair
ford
gland
hear
help
lived
maker
mine
open
rent
rip
shut
slow
son
sort
who
window
wood

STEP 14—*42%*

45%

banker
behind
better
bird
butter
calling
cash
drug
face
found
gone
grant
kid
lady
luck
mail
mate
might
nice
rust
stamp
still
store
table
without

44%
bringing
card
clear
corner
dark
dinner
fishing
mend
north
off
past
rush
show
smart
stone
tend
test
thinking
trust
try
wild
willing
working
yourself

43%
blame
boat
both
close
damp
drum
even
handed
hoping
lives
March
more
new
nose
ours
passing
pole
pools
render
saw
someone
sometime
walk

42%
added
asking
below
bet
cane
cast
class

colder
cooking
football
hand
however
June
leg
lone
lump
nothing
older
once
outfit
river
sixth
stood
these
tile
to-night
winter

41%

bright
drive
felt
fit
fort
glee
hog
inform
lie
master
only
pa
page
park
report
seem
seven
skate
something
start
teaching
wage
walking
whenever
wishing

40%

any
apart
brother
bunch
buy
care
chop
cream
forming
gown

The Iowa Spelling Scales

herself
hour
hunt
hunting
ink
jump
large
longer
looked
loved
lovely
mark
myself
outside
ranch
reader
rice
saved
short
snap
snowed
swell
training
yellow

39%

afternoon
bugs
camp
coy
draft
drill
evening
feeder
getting
goat
handy
having
homesick
horse
I'll
know
lame
leave
lunch
meet
Monday
neck
printing
reading
renting
right
round
Sat.
shed
sock
spelling
summer

wake
worker

38%

alive
backing
Christmas
clay
could
die
done
egg
Feb.
finish
flower
forgive
garment
given
grip
ha
inclose
kitten
least
ma
number
plum
porch
printed
road
rolling
scrap
slide
spend
stick
stunt
washing
yard

STEP 15—34%

37%

across
again
badly
bite
boss
broke
clothing
contest
cost
cross
dandy
eye
farther
fight
frost
fur
great

harder
himself
keeping
market
move
overcoat
paying
sink
staying
storm
train
whatever

36%

case
clock
closer
darling
don't
farmer
filing
forth
hate
held
herewith
inasmuch
need
next
oldest
other
own
pack
rack
rank
roof
sick
sorry
south
suppe
tank
teeth
their
wash
which
won't

35%

air
also
aunt
base
blood
catalogue
chair
chill
church
clean
cooler
cover

deal
fifty
fire
first
fresh
Friday
grit
ground
happen
killed
kinder
kindest
liver
longest
noted
pink
posted
recall
sack
safe
sending
sum
taken
trade
word
write

34%

alone
bean
beg
began
bother
boxes
delay
everyone
feeling
fellow
filling
gift
handsome
hardly
hole
indeed
insist
July
kindly
listed
loud
meal
mostly
mouth
neat
Nov.
Oct.
oil
picking
pride

34 The Iowa Spelling Scales

riding
row
says
shame
shortly
sir
somewhat
space
spending
taking
tiny

33%

bench
called
dice
dose
east
eve
fear
half
holder
house
ill
intend
later
less
mean
meeting
peach
pending
profit
rabbit
remind
renter
sash
saving
soap
spoke
those

32%

adding
agree
ahead
belonging
catch
cattle
check
clever
club
count
covering
dead
deed
dress
every
father
file

flesh
folder
gas
gladly
lighting
likely
linen
making
many
pain
poorly
race
seat
seventh
shade
slept
stage
stating
ton
water
whereby

31%

act
asked
baking
beat
chose
creep
enter
floor
folk
funny
grandma
grind
job
nearer
needing
newspaper
none
pound
protest
sale
shape
smaller
stair
stock
teach
waste
white
woven

STEP 16—27%
30%

another
banking
begun
blew

chairman
change
charge
children
chum
crib
crop
deliver
drew
few
forest
fourth
frame
harvest
herein
hundred
I'm
joke
limit
larger
pair
party
please
post card
scout
showed
sooner
sound
strongly
together
treat
trunk
understanding
washed
weak
wonder

29%

amount
awhile
beef
before
belt
birthday
booklet
brick
closing
dearest
dearly
depend
depending
fail
fix
front
grew
hair
handling
hearing

heat
household
merry
Mrs.
named
payment
per
printer
rained
shipping
thick
thus
true
trying
visit
warm
you'll

28%

add
attending
basket
Bible
brought
brush
calf
cheer
Dr.
drilling
fitting
garden
gee
likewise
manage
mighty
nearly
present
selling
sleet
speed
stranger
sunshine
talking
thankful
track
trained
workmanship

27%

anyone
behalf
block
cared
carpet
carrying
chapter
cleaner
cleaning
cloth

The Iowa Spelling Scales

coffee	unless	kisses	prior
content	wanted	lace	prize
credit	wheel	largest	proper
dare	yesterday	lose	pump
Dec.	yoke	maid	pupil
does	*25%*	member	pure
extent	all right	membership	regard
former	body	o'clock	regret
growing	delighted	oven	remit
housekeeping	dressed	partly	respond
idea	dresser	planted	sand
lining	eight	proud	September
maple	everything	rail	team
nobody	family	removed	throw
opened	glove	rented	understood
packing	heap	sheet	walked
paint	inclosing	shipment	would
self	jar	shoe	*22%*
strike	loss	sire	absent
strongest	lung	started	adjust
sure	mailed	tight	afraid
tax	marking	township	anyway
teacher	maybe	turned	battle
until	overlooked	twice	beaten
wishes	people	use	board
worked	played	wear	chart
26%	queen	wise	copy
admit	renew	won	disposed
always	seal	world	dollar
branch	silver	worth	dream
coal	somewhere		flour
danger	steel	Step 17—21%	forty
December	talk	*23%*	fruit
film	trusting		gain
granted	twenty	almost	glasses
grown	understood	beet	investment
heating	voting	bigger	latest
high	weekly	burn	living
insert	welcome	carry	lowest
isn't	western	closed	lucky
January	wire	cloudy	moved
knew	*24%*	colt	namely
mass	army	deeply	news
month	brain	demand	nineteen
ninth	broken	died	oblige
November	crowd	dirty	per cent
oats	early	enjoying	picture
opening	enjoy	finest	pocket
pencil	filled	fixed	quick
point	fund	greater	seemed
press	handled	grove	simple
program	haven't	inviting	sixty
pull	helpful	main	skating
remark	higher	match	soil
saver	invited	October	stuff
thread	joyful	oversight	toward
tire	kept	plain	tried

turn
velvet
21%
aid
because
birth
bought
cook
crew
daddy
exchange
foolish
frankly
highest
hotel
I'd
inclosed
itself
Latin
latter
loaded
misses
money
moving
nerve
nicely
pretty
setting
submit
taste
tested
third
thought
voter
wrong
20%
agreed
among
attend
brown
busy
buying
coach
dance
dated
death
debate
detail
dwelling
enclosed
enclosing
fare
fever
forenoon
forwarded
goose
grain

habit
hereafter
hereby
iron
I've
junk
knowing
law
load
matter
permit
powder
public
quit
Sept.
since
single
size
standard
supply
title
vote
wagon
wedding
whole
withdraw
wrote
yearly
young
youth
19%
address
ans.
anything
anywhere
blooming
buyer
center
choose
coin
counting
doctor
edge
entry
fact
feel
forwarding
French
friendly
inches
item
join
lumber
mister
monthly
music
perhaps

pillow
plenty
quart
quite
regarding
retail
rushed
seventy
struck
thereafter
travel
tread
Tuesday
upper
watch
wheat

STEP 18–16%

18%
above
ache
adjustment
afloat
already
April
benefit
charming
chicken
closely
company
delayed
discount
dispose
extra
grandfather
greatest
growth
hurt
inspect
invite
joined
laid
mailing
minister
moment
ninety
odd
otherwise
passed
placed
plainly
postage
railroad
reported
sample
Saturday

seller
shown
sickness
sitting
slight
talked
throat
twelve
vary
violin
waited
weather
weigh
whether
writer
Xmas
17%
acting
adopted
artist
attain
cabinet
chain
chance
damage
debating
delivered
else
enjoyed
everybody
fifth
forgotten
globe
haste
hello
independent
informed
known
labor
lamb
lately
leaf
liked
management
needed
person
power
prevent
reaches
ready
recently
refund
rule
sore
study
tatting
ticket

The Iowa Spelling Scales

tired
transit
Tues.
used
worm
zero

16%

advice
advise
agent
auto
await
bottle
country
dancing
didn't
enclose
fern
fifteen
friend
froze
further
greeting
handle
heard
helped
hoped
intended
lesson
loose
lower
message
nurse
owe
range
rapidly
raw
reach
reached
reaching
reply
rubber
sew
square
term
that's
unpaid
utmost
whom
wished
woman

15%

aim
anybody
anyhow
August

awaiting
booster
bottom
branches
building
cheerful
client
comply
devoted
dread
easy
final
finished
follow
fourteen
fully
hasn't
hurry
ideal
island
knot
largely
liberty
locate
lonesome
losing
loving
mistake
outlined
painter
pastor
presented
primary
proved
rainy
raised
repair
return
scare
score
semester
serve
sewing
shock
spare
speak
stayed
suit
temple
therefore
visited
wait
wondering

14%

afterward
ashamed

Aug.
basis
billed
bowl
buggy
captain
cartoon
change
changing
cleaned
clerk
clothe
control
county
covered
dealing
delightful
elect
expert
failed
flavor
fullest
gasoline
germ
gotten
gravy
hardware
hare
improve
inst.
kindness
ladies
loan
lonely
manual
mere
method
missed
office
ordering
packed
placing
provided
quickly
renewed
respect
ribbon
serving
should
slightly
smooth
speaker
stated
steam
thanksgiving
thereof
unable

uncle
useful
value
waiting
wearing
weary
wouldn't

STEP 19–12%

13%

alfalfa
aren't
boiler
booth
bushel
charged
classes
clearly
confined
constant
dozen
eager
extend
fairly
fancy
greatly
industry
learn
learned
leaves
level
lovingly
model
movement
needle
noise
owing
patent
pavement
pleased
proof
recent
recovered
remembering
served
share
slipper
taught
thousand
topic
wasn't
watching
women
you'd
zone

12%

answered
apply
beyond
breaking
build
candle
caught
checking
choosing
coasting
color
comfort
cough
decline
dependent
desire
earth
eighty
eleventh
enrollment
fence
forward
freeze
friendship
furnish
gaining
guess
health
hence
illness
installed
interest
ivory
leader
letting
located
manner
meantime
northern
obliged
offering
organ
ought
owned
patch
performed
problem
providing
quarter
rapid
record
refuse
request
rifle
safety
season

second
server
settle
skirt
soldier
tract
using
voice
Wednesday

11%

advantage
agreeable
amendment
backed
bluff
careful
carefully
cause
caused
colored
cottage
court
cute
delivery
disgusted
during
enough
entirely
express
February
federal
formed
formerly
graze
heavy
history
interested
interesting
manager
modern
nevertheless
notion
offered
painted
parlor
penny
piano
picnic
post office
prevented
promotion
prompt
promptly
proves
putting
raising

recover
relation
remove
scale
spirit
splendid
steady
stopped
strict
subject
suffering
talent
tanning
taxes
to-morrow
truly
we'll
witch
worry

10%

abstract
advising
against
allow
ankle
answer
answering
applicant
automobile
Ave.
awful
barley
bridge
Bro.
button
cheap
coast
collar
condition
crazy
democrat
destroyed
due
ease
enroll
entitle
field
furnishing
gallon
gentleman
hadn't
heretofore
important
including
information
invoice

kitchen
leaving
length
limb
madam
married
middle
misunderstanding
ordered
painting
preparing
properly
publisher
quiet
quote
reason
refer
remember
represented
result
several
simply
spread
stamped
studying
supplied
text
Thursday
trace
wonderful
X-ray

STEP 20—8%

9%

acre
addresses
advance
advertising
appeal
attach
attached
bass
boarding
broad
candidate
carried
cheaper
confident
consist
contain
contained
containing
continue
convince
cotton
credited

The Iowa Spelling Scales

customer	united	relative	graduation
daily	vacation	renewal	grammar
dairy	valued	republican	guide
data	view	reputation	heir
dealer	whose	returning	homestead
degree	writing	satisfy	honest
deportment	yourselves	shipped	human
direct	*8%*	shipper	hurried
discontinued	addressed	sign	improved
duty	advertise	situation	increasing
employed	ample	statement	jury
enrolled	argument	station	justify
entertainment	assist	sugar	learning
except	assortment	surprise	leather
favor	attention	thesis	librarian
firm	barely	though	limited
following	believe	touch	listen
fortune	blackberries	towel	literary
girlie	braid	visiting	location
happened	builder	waist	loyal
improving	built	we've	merit
instant	bulk	winner	obtain
instructed	cellar	*7%*	operation
intention	comfortable	ability	patron
internal	confer	according	perfect
international	continued	acted	perfectly
machine	daughter	active	piece
nation	education	addition	policy
normal	effort	adjusted	prepaid
ocean	establish	administrator	property
pattern	etc.	ambition	published
peace	figure	auntie	question
phone	fuel	between	register
phoned	gained	bracelet	regular
potatoes	gentlemen	break	regulation
postal	German	breakfast	remedy
prefer	good-bye	capital	remembered
president	grateful	cashier	rendered
promised	healthy	checked	resident
proven	meter	concluded	section
raise	officer	consider	seldom
reasonable	opera	considerable	shopping
remain	operated	contract	shoulder
replying	package	conversation	style
represent	payable	cutting	suppose
requested	pearl	desired	thirty
returned	planning	develop	total
ruin	pleasant	director	transfer
running	position	discovered	treated
rye	priced	dodge	vacant
student	Prof.	drama	valley
suggest	protected	entire	
support	provide	exceptional	STEP 21—*6%*
through	queer	explained	*6%*
trouble	raiser	fault	account
turkey	realize	fitted	action
uniform	reduce	force	actor

The Iowa Spelling Scales

advertisement	ourselves	convinced	submitted
allowed	personal	correct	suggested
although	planned	course	suitable
altogether	popular	deserve	supposed
appear	possess	district	terrible
applied	possibly	doesn't	tickled
appointment	prayer	doubt	volume
average	preacher	earnest	watched
avoid	product	employee	
ballot	prospect	entertaining	STEP 22—4%
based	really	ere	
believing	realizing	estimated	*4%*
blessed	repeat	example	absolute
calendar	require	expected	absolutely
cherries	retain	explain	accept
choice	route	explaining	accordance
college	saddle	federation	advised
common	sanitary	female	alley
complete	satisfactory	foundation	appearance
congratulate	secure	general	appointed
consideration	secured	group	arrive
contemplated	separate	hauled	arrived
convention	settlement	headache	assuring
copies	silence	honestly	bonus
corporation	slippery	illustrated	butcher
correspondent	studies	include	canvass
couple	subscriber	included	capacity
cousin	surprised	invitation	carrier
curtain	throughout	lbs.	certain
decide	traveling	lodge	circular
decided	treatment	maintain	compelled
desiring	trial	mentioned	constantly
earning	weight	million	correction
eighteen	weren't	minute	crippled
either	worrying	moral	cure
election	worse	narrow	democratic
English	worst	noticed	deposit
entered	*5%*	opinion	depot
envelope	advertised	owner	described
examination	affair	particular	directed
favorite	amounting	parties	disappointment
figured	attractive	personality	disposal
forced	beauty	pertaining	earliest
graduating	biggest	possible	elected
hesitate	calm	preparation	entitled
holiday	cement	prepared	evidently
honor	central	private	exactly
hospital	chief	quoted	exam.
husband	cigar	reliable	excuse
ironing	cities	reliability	exhibit
judge	combination	requesting	expired
label	commence	reserve	expensive
mention	conduct	salary	expressed
neglect	congratulation	select	fabric
notice	consequently	service	factory
notify	considered	sorrow	failure
orange	considering	stories	future

The Iowa Spelling Scales

genuine
graduate
guest
handkerchief
happiness
headquarter
immense
improvement
inclined
increase
inquire
inquiry
instead
instruct
investigation
jobber
judgment
laugh
lecture
legal
library
local
manufacture
meant
merely
nature
neighbor
neighborhood
nervous
nickel
obligation
obtained
practical
practicing
procured
produce
progress
purchase
purpose
quality
receive
reference
referring
refreshment
refused
required
respectfully
satisfied
search
settled
signature
signed
special
surface
sweater
theater
treasurer

union
urge
valuable
welfare
worthy
written

3%

absence
accomplish
accommodate
acquainted
administration
adventure
agriculture
allotment
animal
anxious
application
appreciated
arrange
arranged
article
assembly
assistant
athletics
attended
author
automatic
available
awfully
balance
banquet
bargain
brief
bulletin
burden
business
carnival
cedar
certainly
climate
collect
completely
composition
concern
confirming
connected
connection
conveniently
co-operating
couldn't
council
crowded
debt
difference
difficulty
direction

disease
distribution
division
dreadful
durable
easily
employer
entering
epidemic
equipped
error
especially
established
excellent
excited
exciting
expense
explanation
extensive
factor
factories
favorable
favored
feature
figuring
freight
frequently
frozen
furnace
furnished
garage
geometry
ghost
guarantee
guaranteed
imagine
increased
identify
indicate
inducement
immediately
installment
instance
institution
investigate
involved
journal
justified
knowledge
magazine
material
materially
measure
mortgage
national
naturally
object

occupied
operating
ordinary
organization
organized
original
parcel
parent
period
practically
practice
premium
prepare
presume
principal
principle
privilege
probably
proceed
profitable
promise
publication
rec'd
received
recommend
referred
regardless
relieve
requirement
reservation
response
resulting
Sabbath
salesman
satisfaction
satisfactory
secretary
securing
sense
society
straight
subscription
superintendent
surplus
telephone
thorough
thoroughly
timothy
usually

Step 23—2%

accordingly
additional
affectionately
annual
annually

anticipating
appendicitis
arrival
assessment
assure
assured
attempt
attendance
authorized
aware
beginning
canned
capable
certificate
chautauqua
Christian
circulation
circuit
circus
citizen
civics
coarse
collection
commission
commissioner
committee
communication
companion
complaint
concerning
concert
confidence
connected
connecting
conservatory
consultation
contemplating
contrary
co-operative
correctly
courage
creamery
current
cushion
customary
definite
deliveries
demonstrated
deserved
development
different
directly
domestic
doubtless
duties
effect
electrical

elsewhere
engineer
engineering
entertain
equipment
excess
exclusively
executive
exercise
exhibition
existing
experience
expression
extreme
fashion
finally
followed
fraternally
funeral
geography
glorious
gratitude
grocery
Hallowe'en
honorable
illustration
importance
impossible
influence
inquiries
inspector
insurance
interfere
issue
junior
language
legislation
liable
liberal
literature
machinery
medicine
mental
merchandise
moderate
musical
neglected
nephew
niece
organize
pardon
patient
permanent
politics
positive
preliminary
presence

production
proposition
purchased
qualities
quantity
readily
receiving
recess
recite
reduction
registered
registration
remembrance
representation
responsible
rough
rural
selected
senior
similar
sincere
social
solicit
strawberries
succeeded
success
successful
superior
supervision
system
telegram
territory
themselves
transportation
university
variety
weighed
wholesale
worried

STEP 24—1%

accident
accomplished
accredited
acknowledge
actual
actually
admission
advanced
advancement
algebra
analysis
anniversary
announce
appeared
appreciate

appreciation
approved
arriving
assigned
assignment
assistance
associated
association
assume
assurance
attraction
authority
avenue
barrel
calves
campaign
candidacy
celebrate
channel
choir
circumstances
commerce
commercial
community
companies
conclusion
conference
confirm
connect
consequence
considerably
constitution
construction
convenience
co-operation
cordial
cordially
corrected
correspond
crochet
crocheting
coupon
dangerous
decision
decrease
definitely
design
destination
discourage
duplicate
efficiency
efficient
electricity
enormous
enthusiasm
enthusiastic
essential

evidence
examine
examined
examiner
exception
exceptionally
exhausted
expecting
extended
extension
famous
fashionable
favorably
fierce
financial
furniture
generous
government
gradually
grippe
hastily
humor
hustling
illustrating
immediate
impression
inconvenience
individual
institute
instruction
instructor
instrument
introduced
introduction
issued
license
lieutenant
liquid
mechanical
necessary
necessity
neither
notary
notified
numerous
official

opportunity
orchestra
originally
particularly
physician
pneumonia
politician
possession
previous
produced
prosperity
receipt
reception
reduced
regretting
regularly
relationship
relieved
remained
remittance
representative
resigned
resource
scarce
science
selection
series
serious
sincerely
soliciting
specially
stationary
stomach
straightened
strength
strictly
struggle
studied
substitute
succeed
sufficient
supervisor
supplies
surgery
sympathy
tuberculosis

type
universal
unusually
usual
vision
zephyr

STEP 25—0%

acceptance
accompanying
acquaintance
acquire
activity
advisable
affidavit
agency
agricultural
alumni
ambitious
announcement
anticipate
apparatus
appreciating
approval
arrangement
associate
attitude
attorney
auditor
blizzard
bureau
character
characteristic
collecting
compliment
confirmation
continuous
convenient
correspondence
courteous
demonstration
description
difficult
disagreeable
disappoint

disappointed
encourage
equally
exact
excitement
executed
extremely
familiar
foreign
fortunate
fundamental
generally
inferior
ingredients
leisure
majority
manufacturing
maturity
mountain
natural
occasion
occasionally
peculiarities
personally
phosphorus
physical
possibility
prevail
process
profession
professional
prosperous
qualities
quotation
recommendation
responsibility
rheumatism
schedule
scientific
source
specification
unnecessary
unusual
various
vicinity

SECTION X

THE IOWA SPELLING SCALE

GRADE III

GRADE III

STEP 1—100%
in

STEP 2—99%
is

STEP 3—98%
are
good
he
it

STEP 4—96%

97%
can
my
see
that

96%
and
be
book
day
she

STEP 5—94%

95%
all
at
but
did
do
little
not
out
was
you

94%
dear
dog
eat
go
me
old
to-day
year

STEP 6—92%

93%
ice
will

92%
by
come
get
have
into
may
on
one
play
say
time
with
your

91%
an
for
his
like
man
some
the
them
up
way

STEP 7—88%

90%
big
gold
got
had
her
of
over
think
this
tree
wood

89%
ask
give
how
if
land
last
let
look
love
tell
ten
then

88%
being

boy
cannot
hand
run
sent
we

87%
ago
as
down
home
so
toy
when

STEP 8—84%

86%
age
bell
door
from
letter
live
night
or
red
thing
till
us

85%
bee
box
came
coat
forget
going
most
three
throat
well
what

84%
apple
bad
cat
fast
fish
grade
hat
king
light
long

looking
make
much
must
pay
put
sand
sat
six
snow
sun
yet

83%
after
bed
bring
cold
cow
far
foot
ill
just
kill
made
meat
they
top
week

82%
back
ball
black
call
doing
five
gave
grass
green
hard
has
ink
lot
mother
Mr.
playing
ring
ship
Sunday
tent
thank
there
wind

46

The Iowa Spelling Scales

STEP 9—79%

81%
about
am
baby
bank
bay
best
each
feet
fill
food
hill
him
inside
lay
May
more
seeing
send
sheep
without
work
yes

80%
away
boat
butter
cake
cent
cut
ever
free
lost
Monday
morning
new
no
pig
place
read
stove
sweet
went
west
working

79%
become
child
hen
milk
name
pie
poor
rich
school

singing
tenth
too
town
war

78%
along
aside
car
colder
face
fat
girl
goat
hall
house
lake
late
left
March
off
oil
once
rain
same
stay
take
very

77%
backing
band
belong
blow
cup
end
fell
fine
flower
fun
grand
hay
its
mad
now
nut
overcoat
papa
part
pine
ride
rust
side
silk
sister
snowing
son

song
soon
spell
standing
start
state
told
two
under
want
why
within

STEP 10—73%

76%
add
bear
calling
card
care
corn
fall
find
four
happy
hear
hold
joy
keep
kind
longer
low
never
park
pen
pin
plan
room
seed
sleep
spelling
sport
stone
summer
upon
where

75%
able
around
banker
cover
dad
every
farm
Friday
game

glad
here
hunt
mine
note
sad
shop
sold
stand
stop
table
thanking
to-night
wall
win

74%
bid
cap
eye
Feb.
first
flat
help
hot
Jan.
Miss
nice
our
pink
print
real
said
saw
seen
spent
to
willing
yard

73%
better
bill
east
forget
goldfish
lived
lives
many
myself
net
nine
noon
open
river
rock
set
show
sick

soft	washing	step	those
window	wish	test	took
winter	*70%*	wanting	walking
72%	afternoon	*68%*	which
any	barn	arm	white
baker	became	asking	write
blue	can't	bat	yellow
city	children	behind	*66%*
cook	cream	below	adding
dance	deep	brand	air
die	drive	bright	alive
dinner	dust	danger	belonging
gate	faster	dark	cane
head	father	fair	cattle
helping	gray	feed	clock
inch	heat	fit	coming
kiss	hit	June	done
maker	hog	lady	don't
mate	hour	lone	fire
mill	large	mail	ford
near	mark	north	form
older	mud	nothing	garden
paper	oh	order	gather
picking	outside	race	handed
post	page	rolling	holding
rent	price	sin	kindly
rose	rest	sit	leave
shot	round	spot	ma
store	sell	starting	making
thin	spring	teach	market
tip	train	teacher	meal
were	true	thinking	pa
who	trust	try	paying
wide	water	walk	reading
71%	wife	yourself	report
bird		*67%*	stamp
brother	STEP 11—66%	art	whatever
date	*69%*	banking	*65%*
even		been	added
felt	ate	blank	author
finding	beside	both	bet
forgive	bit	clay	born
found	clear	Dec.	bunch
gone	close	fort	cool
kid	cost	glass	hers
landing	could	hair	hunting
life	dress	however	income
pick	drop	master	January
plow	fishing	Nov.	lame
seven	given	plate	met
slow	ground	Sat.	mind
stage	Oct.	seat	move
still	other	shut	right
stood	rate	something	rush
supper	road	stick	sending
telling	rug	street	sort
	saying	teeth	south

The Iowa Spelling Scales

such
talk
wake
wild
    64%
ahead
bean
buy
camp
cash
class
delay
drum
feeding
handy
horse
later
lift
neck
next
pack
peach
rank
short
slip
snowed
storm
these
wet
    63%
also
brick
cast
clean
cooking
cord
dandy
display
flour
fur
ha
held
indeed
mouth
nap
roof
sound
spend
taking
track

STEP 12—58%
    62%
bringing
draft
eight

eve
farmer
fear
few
fight
finger
July
longest
luck
mean
news
nose
own
party
per
poorly
reader
rice
sack
safe
sink
sir
smart
tank
tend
thereafter
tiny
trip
weak
wishing
would
    61%
another
April
asleep
blame
brush
chair
coal
contest
corner
dead
deal
dearly
died
fellow
hang
hardly
hearing
herself
hole
inasmuch
kinder
know
larger
list
miss

nor
ours
pass
past
pencil
please
porch
post card
posted
rail
raining
saved
shoe
small
space
sugar
than
their
whenever
worker
yearly
    60%
always
apart
asked
bite
block
body
cloth
count
cross
dream
fifty
football
great
job
loved
month
nearly
need
none
outfit
queen
shipment
sunshine
tie
Tuesday
wise
won't
yesterday
    59%
across
afloat
beat
begin
blood
farming

harder
holder
jump
kitten
looked
meet
October
only
pain
pillow
pole
roll
sis
sixty
someone
staying
taken
talking
while
wonder
wool
    58%
army
case
chop
church
darling
December
everything
forest
gift
glove
goose
half
happen
having
high
leaves
matter
pound
rained
seem
shade
shall
soap
sorry
stated
teaching
thought
twenty
wash
word
world
    57%
agree
alone
anyone

anything
basket
bench
content
egg
filling
fix
frost
fruit
grant
growing
kindest
lie
liver
money
oven
peace
reach
renew
row
self
should
skate
slide
stock
warm
wheel

56%

again
aunt
belt
called
carpet
check
clothing
damp
enter
floor
gladly
law
marking
Mrs.
nobody
oats
orange
pocket
printed
protest
rabbit
renter
silver
third
thread
thus
tile
wishes

55%

birthday
Christmas
cleaning
closer
evening
gland
grandma
hundred
lace
least
noted
number
otherwise
pair
planted
plum
pull
pure
quart
ranch
saver
sew
snap
sometime
speed
spending
tested
worked

STEP 13—50%

54%

badly
because
bought
brought
cheer
chill
club
covering
crop
dearest
drill
everyone
fee
grandfather
himself
inclose
invited
itself
leg
less
load
lump
might
November

oldest
packing
passing
point
ready
recall
rented
riding
rod
says
sight
somewhat
sore
stranger
swell
township
treat
use
wanted
washed

53%

boxes
branch
chart
earth
farther
folk
grain
I'll
inform
keeping
mend
mostly
penny
powder
pride
quick
render
saving
selling
sheet
sooner
team
training
trusting
welcome
wheat
whereby
worth

52%

above
battle
begun
cared
chain
charge
closed

color
creep
deed
dresser
heating
homesick
hoping
island
leader
learn
maid
oblige
opened
overlooked
rack
shape
spoke
stunt
thankful
trade
wage
Wednesday

51%

bother
bugs
carry
counting
country
crib
deliver
early
easy
eighty
finish
folder
former
forth
greeting
hate
hereafter
lovely
lumber
mailed
mamma
paint
person
proper
proud
railroad
shed
soil
steam
study
thick
throw
twice
unless

The Iowa Spelling Scales

wagon
youth
50%
booklet
brown
candle
depend
does
grew
grind
intend
killed
lighting
lose
maple
meeting
nearer
opening
payment
pools
pretty
remark
seventy
stair
understanding
walked
weekly
young
49%
all right
bog
boss
bottle
brain
busy
coffee
colt
doctor
fence
file
forty
fresh
glee
granted
handle
I'm
lunch
moving
partly
people
printing
renting
September
seventh
sixth
size

tire
trying
48%
anyhow
before
Bible
broke
copy
coy
drew
feeder
front
heard
herewith
higher
hoped
household
listed
match
mister
moment
picture
post office
remind
rule
seal
shame
speak
stating
sum
tax
ticket
turn
wear
47%
catch
change
cleaner
clever
death
dread
drug
garment
gee
gown
iron
knew
main
member
merry
moved
needing
nineteen
remove
rip
sash
scrap

speaker
ton
travel
trunk
used
velvet
wire
46%
afraid
almost
began
behalf
between
chicken
closing
dice
enjoy
fail
fifteen
flesh
frame
funny
grip
grown
inclosed
junk
kindness
kisses
laugh
lesson
liberty
living
maybe
named
neat
painted
pleased
printer
shortly
strongest
watch
won
woven

STEP 14—42%
45%
ans.
anyway
blew
branches
broken
buying
demand
French
getting
grove

housekeeping
invite
inviting
leaf
learned
liked
loaded
loud
painter
pending
played
pleasure
plenty
press
reached
simple
sleet
Thursday
together
tried
unable
waited
weather
woman
wrong
44%
beet
board
calf
cleaned
company
cotton
dare
Dr.
everybody
feeling
filled
gas
harvest
improve
inches
joke
joyful
largest
likewise
membership
newspaper
odd
pump
regard
regret
retail
rubber
scout
sewing
sock
somewhere

started
strike
turkey
voter
western
writing
wrote

43%
auto
charming
chose
dated
drilling
enclosed
filing
finest
handling
helpful
hurt
I'd
idea
insist
latter
leather
lower
mighty
office
plain
present
quite
recover
removed
running
smaller
that's
Tues.

42%
afterward
amount
birth
classes
friend
glasses
globe
grip
handsome
hurry
learning
needed
patch
postage
quickly
return
Saturday
second
Sept.

sure
twelve
understand
worm
you'll

41%
act
agent
among
ashamed
Aug.
Ave.
awhile
cause
chairman
cooler
delighted
extent
fourth
fully
heat
herein
jar
likely
loving
music
phone
potatoes
power
prize
profit
prove
range
reaching
respond
sale
sample
steel
until
wedding
women

40%
already
answer
anybody
anywhere
boiler
burn
chance
cloudy
dose
dozen
dressed
fifth
follow
frankly
fund

gallon
hardware
insert
knowing
known
latest
meantime
monthly
nation
program
raw
settle
sitting
slipper
taste
trace
waiting
whom
writer
Xmas.

39%
address
beef
beg
chum
crowd
damage
discount
duty
feel
knot
linen
loss
manage
packed
painting
perhaps
remit
retain
since
slept
suit
therefore
title
uncle
visit
vote
workmanship

38%
baking
bushel
coin
cottage
debate
gotten
greater
limb

lonely
noise
regarding
reply
reported
seller
sickness
utmost
weary
wished

STEP 15—34%

37%
base
building
buyer
coach
comply
deeply
delightful
dirty
during
fact
fairly
forward
guess
hare
heavy
hereby
history
informed
join
listen
manner
minute
movement
namely
ordering
organ
ought
payable
prevent
provided
quit
reason
remain
seemed
skating
thereof
tight
trained
whole
witch
withdraw
worst

The Iowa Spelling Scales

36%

adjust
backed
bottom
buggy
button
catalogue
caused
checking
clearly
county
cutting
dancing
depending
eighteen
field
friendly
further
habit
isn't
lamb
leaving
lucky
mailing
misses
mistake
nerve
nevertheless
owing
pearl
proved
quarter
ribbon
setting
showed
spread
talked
Thanksgiving
tired
tread
treated
wait
watching

35%

August
awaiting
bigger
bulk
center
chapter
daily
enclosing
express
failed
family
fixed
haven't
highest
inclosing
outlined
placing
remember
serve
share
single
skirt
strongly
thirty
toward
visiting

34%

advise
agreed
break
Bro.
choose
coast
court
devoted
dollar
figure
film
frozen
gravy
handled
kept
letting
performed
repeat
scale
shopping
submit
through
value

33%

carrying
changing
collar
daddy
dealing
dispose
edge
fancy
fever
fitting
forwarded
illness
intended
kitchen
lung
mass
obliged
o'clock
permit
raised
rushed
score
shoulder
soldier
waist
waste
wonderful
zone

32%

acting
build
builder
changed
comfort
debating
delivered
desire
disposed
eleventh
enough
exchange
fourteen
froze
fullest
gum
greatest
homestead
independent
inspect
labor
lowest
needle
nicely
ninth
officer
oversight
owe
placed
providing
quiet
reaches
server
shone
simply
square
stuff
though
understood
voting
whether

31%

absent
await
beaten
clerk
crazy
earning
elect
expert
extra
finished
forgotten
formed
forwarding
hotel
item
I've
level
lining
lonesome
narrow
ninety
parlor
picnic
proof
recovered
returned
season
served
shipping
thousand
truly
upper

Step 16—27%

30%

advice
barrel
broad
careful
caught
charged
cheaper
cheerful
credit
eager
else
enclose
enjoying
February
foolish
helped
invoice
nickel
nurse
plainly
provide
raising
recite
record
scare

sign
slight
struck
vacation
worry
29%
admit
alfalfa
answered
breakfast
checked
cherries
covered
dealer
enjoyed
explain
extend
German
laid
Latin
losing
pavement
per cent
prevented
proven
queer
raise
recent
recess
remembering
request
rough
sire
smooth
supply
temple
to-morrow
turned
unpaid
using
worse
yoke
28%
built
cheap
colored
consist
decline
delayed
fern
gain
haste
ideal
joined
ladies
locate
lovingly

middle
notice
passed
patent
phoned
pupil
putting
repair
saddle
stayed
studying
taught
taxes
touch
united
valued
voice
we'll
27%
addresses
aid
attend
blessed
booth
bridge
carefully
coasting
confined
contain
detail
entry
factory
furnishing
happened
holiday
including
instead
investment
largely
loose
ocean
respect
returning
ruin
secure
standard
statement
suffering
surprise
throughout
useful
vary
violin
zero
26%
aim
amounting

artist
beyond
bowl
closely
continue
contract
cure
delivery
dreadful
ease
explained
favor
force
gaining
gentleman
graze
health
hence
honest
improving
limit
married
preacher
properly
public
refund
serving
shock
spare
stamped
trouble
watched
wearing
wondering
25%
acted
amply
ankle
answering
balance
barley
blooming
captain
clothe
common
control
cough
crew
dairy
didn't
either
entering
excuse
forenoon
good-bye
greatly
instant

loan
offering
package
perfect
piano
problem
promise
rainy
recently
renewed
requested
stories
towel
24%
active
adjustment
billed
circus
cousin
cripple
dodge
figured
friendship
furnish
hasn't
hello
industry
inst.
interesting
lately
management
mention
model
obtained
ordered
owned
primary
prior
property
rapid
refuse
suitable
text
whose
wouldn't

STEP 17—21%
23%
advance
aren't
breaking
carried
cellar
contained
containing
explaining

The Iowa Spelling Scales

formerly	entertaining	prompt	tatting
freeze	entire	quoted	uniform
gentlemen	ere	rapidly	worrying
group	etc.	receive	
guide	except	refreshment	STEP 18—16%
headquarter	flavor	rendered	
interest	following	replying	18%
language	hurried	require	addressed
manager	improved	search	attain
message	jury	silence	avenue
pastor	maintain	situation	avoid
postal	method	splendid	butcher
presented	owner	stopped	cartoon
slightly	promised	weigh	climate
sorrow	represented		companion
talent	strict	19%	couple
treatment	suppose	advising	described
	tract	apply	employed
22%	traveling	argument	enrollment
abstract	visited	booster	example
actor	wasn't	cigar	final
animal	winner	confident	information
attending	written	creamery	intention
bluff	you'd	due	interested
boarding	yourselves	favorite	lecture
dependent		fortune	lodge
earnest	20%	fuel	mentioned
enroll	addition	furnace	notion
entered	adjusted	furnished	offered
fare	advantage	guest	operated
firm	advertised	handkerchief	popular
headache	alley	husband	prepared
healthy	aware	important	procured
pattern	beauty	include	Prof.
publisher	cabinet	included	prospect
rye	client	installed	raiser
seldom	constant	ironing	refused
steady	convention	jobber	republican
studies	decided	minister	reserve
surface	deportment	normal	safety
term	deserve	obtain	semester
transit	direct	planning	settled
	dwelling	pleasant	slippery
21%	enrolled	promotion	spirit
adopted	female	protected	
against	figuring	question	17%
agreeable	fitted	realize	although
allow	gained	refer	benefit
amendment	growth	represent	biggest
attach	honestly	required	calm
automobile	honor	satisfied	carrier
bass	increasing	**select**	comfortable
believe	limited	settlement	condition
burden	located	several	democrat
chief	machine	station	desiring
degree	missed	student	**effort**
desired	modern	subject	election
discovered	northern	support	entertainment
English			

expressed	theater	separate	doubt
fault	tickled	valley	exciting
grocery	topic	*14%*	extended
hadn't	vacant	adventure	famous
human	we've	advertise	followed
instructed	*15%*	affair	foundation
ivory	advertisement	applied	freight
length	advertising	assist	general
local	altogether	auntie	girlie
loyal	appear	barely	graduating
nature	based	basis	graduation
piece	bracelet	candidate	heir
prepaid	canned	capable	inclined
produce	choice	capital	inspector
really	combination	concluded	location
relation	correct	conduct	meant
rifle	customer	confer	parcel
shipper	cute	consideration	period
sweater	destroyed	continued	personal
weighed	district	copies	positive
16%	drama	course	prefer
ambition	entitle	excited	production
average	equally	expecting	realizing
bargain	expired	factor	salary
blackberries	gasoline	fashion	sanitary
consider	importance	forced	satisfaction
considering	increased	judge	secured
contemplated	international	library	selection
conversation	madam	manufacture	stomach
daughter	manual	operation	success
decide	measure	parent	telegram
depot	meter	product	telephone
directed	misunderstanding	quote	total
direction	moral	relative	welfare
director	mountain	reputation	worthy
discontinued	neglect	Sabbath	*12%*
disgusted	neither	studied	advanced
doesn't	object	style	assure
education	organized	tanning	attention
entirely	ourselves	view	believing
federal	pardon	weight	central
future	perfectly		coarse
garage	president	Step 19—12%	college
grateful	publication		complaint
inquiry	published	*13%*	complete
lbs.	purpose	ache	congratulation
parties	reasonable	action	considered
patron	reduction	advised	constantly
pertaining	regardless	appointment	contrary
prayer	relationship	arrange	convince
promptly	renewal	braid	different
result	requesting	certainly	duties
route	resident	choosing	easily
service	resulting	considerable	elected
shipped	salesman	couldn't	equipment
struggle	satisfactory	credited	exam.
surprised	scarce	disposal	existing

expected
failure
favorable
heretofore
inquire
invitation
justify
literary
niece
personality
preparation
prepare
priced
produced
regular
remedy
respectfully
responsible
sense
signed
strawberries
superintendent
transfer
X-ray
11%
ability
appeal
athletics
awful
calendar
capacity
cedar
concern
concert
conference
congratulate
correction
courage
curtain
duplicate
durable
employee
entertain
evidently
explanation
ghost
identify
increase
installment
institution
label
liquid
mere
opera
position
possess
possible

progress
reference
register
remembered
section
straight
surplus
themselves
10%
absolute
according
agency
appeared
applicant
arrived
attached
automatic
beginning
cement
commence
concerning
convinced
co-operating
corporation
crowded
data
develop
directly
engineer
envelope
exactly
exhibit
fabric
grammar
happiness
hesitate
hospital
indicate
influence
instruct
internal
investigation
justified
million
neglected
nephew
noticed
policy
presume
private
proposition
rec'd
reduced
registered
regulation
reliable
securing

suggested
treasurer
trial
valuable
volume
worried

STEP 20—8%.

9%
absolutely
account
administrator
arrive
assured
banquet
certain
choir
companies
composition
confirming
deliveries
democratic
deserved
distribution
earliest
elsewhere
establish
established
examination
extensive
factories
funeral
genuine
geography
hauled
honorable
improvement
neighborhood
nervous
obligation
organize
practice
quality
received
registration
reliability
relieve
selected
strength
subscriber
thesis
thorough
union
8%
absence
acre

arranged
article
assuring
attended
attraction
attractive
calves
canvass
carnival
cashier
Christian
cities
collect
connect
connected
consequently
council
current
deposit
description
design
disappointment
entitled
exception
favored
instance
involved
literature
machinery
merit
mortgage
ordinary
particular
preliminary
preparing
prevail
proceed
recommend
representation
requirement
resigned
satisfactorily
satisfy
secretary
signature
suggest
supplied
supplies
universal
7%
additional
allowed
application
assistant
attempt
authorized
brief

The Iowa Spelling Scales

channel
collection
completely
confidence
connection
co-operation
cushion
dangerous
debt
destination
difference
division
employer
exact
exceptional
excitement
exercise
expense
expensive
expression
extreme
feature
fraternally
furniture
graduate
hastily
illustrated
inducement
instruction
insurance
introduced
legal
legislation
magazine
medicine
musical
national
notary
notify
occupied
operating
opinion
organization
patient
permanent
possibly
practical
probably
profession
receiving
reception
reduce
remembrance
reservation
rural
special
straightened

submitted
supposed
terrible
urge
weren't
wholesale

STEP 21—6%

6%

accept
accomplish
agriculture
announce
assigned
assortment
ballot
bulletin
celebrate
circuit
circular
collecting
communication
community
compelled
confirm
correspond
correspondent
decrease
demonstrated
disagreeable
engineering
error
estimated
evidence
excess
experience
fierce
frequently
geometry
gratitude
guaranteed
hustling
imagine
junior
knowledge
material
mental
merchandise
merely
neighbor
numerous
original
planned
quantity
referring
remittance
representative

similar
society
succeeded
university
variety
vision

5%

accordance
acknowledge
acquire
allotment
alumni
anniversary
anxious
attorney
available
awfully
bonus
citizen
commerce
committee
constitution
contemplating
conveniently
correctly
correspondence
coupon
difficulty
domestic
doubtless
effect
electrical
examine
exclusively
fashionable
federation
generally
glorious
government
humor
illustrating
immediate
immediately
impossible
inconvenience
inquires
issue
issued
judgment
liable
liberal
moderate
notified
occasion
official
politics
principle

privilege
process
prosperous
readily
regularly
serious
social
subscription
successful
surgery
sympathy
timothy
type
usual

STEP 22—4%

4%

acceptance
accident
acquainted
actual
advancement
affectionately
algebra
annual
appearance
appointed
appreciated
assignment
assistance
assume
assurance
blizzard
bureau
business
certificate
character
circulation
circumstances
conclusion
connecting
conservatory
considerably
convenience
cordially
crocheting
customary
decision
definitely
development
disease
efficient
electricity
enthusiasm
epidemic
examined

excellent
executed
executive
exhausted
familiar
finally
generous
illustration
instructor
investigate
journal
materially
naturally
opportunity
personally
physician
practically
premium
principal
profitable
purchased
qualities
quotation
recommendation
referred
response
science
series
sincere
strictly
succeed
sufficient
superior
system
thoroughly
transportation
unusually
various

3%

accommodate
accordingly
activity
affidavit
approval
approved
arrangement
arrival
arriving
assessment
association

attendance
civics
convenient
cordial
corrected
definite
difficult
disappoint
discourage
efficiency
encourage
enormous
equipped
especially
examiner
exhibition
extension
favorably
guarantee
impression
instrument
interfere
librarian
manufacturing
practicing
presence
purchase
receipt
relieved
remained
sincerely
solicit
specification
stationary
supervision
territory
usually
vicinity
zephyr

STEP 23—2%

accompanying
accredited
actually
administration
admission
agricultural
announcement
anticipating

appreciate
assembly
auditor
authority
campaign
candidacy
commercial
commission
commissioner
compliment
consequence
construction
consultation
co-operative
crochet
demonstration
disappointed
enthusiastic
financial
gradually
grippe
immense
inferior
institute
introduced
lieutenant
mechanical
natural
necessity
originally
particularly
previous
professional
prosperity
regretting
rheumatism
source
substitute
supervisor
unnecessary
unusual

STEP 24—1%

accomplished
acquaintance
ambitious
analysis
annually

apparatus
appendicitis
appreciation
associate
associated
attitude
characteristic
chautauqua
confirmation
continuous
courteous
exceptionally
extremely
fundamental
Hallowe'en
individual
ingredients
leisure
majority
maturity
necessary
orchestra
pneumonia
politician
possibility
quantities
resource
responsibility
schedule
senior
soliciting
specially

STEP 25—0%

advisable
anticipate
appreciating
essential
foreign
fortunate
license
occasionally
peculiarities
phosphorus
physical
possession
scientific
tuberculosis

SECTION XI

THE IOWA SPELLING SCALE

GRADE IV

GRADE IV

STEP 1—100%
- all
- at
- did
- dog
- me
- thank
- thing
- to-day

STEP 2—99%
- and
- are
- big
- book
- but
- day
- dear
- good
- have
- he
- his
- is
- it
- land
- like
- little
- look
- May
- out
- run
- see
- ship
- tree
- up
- was
- what
- year
- you

STEP 3—98%
- as
- away
- be
- boy
- can
- come
- each
- get
- give
- go
- got
- hand
- in
- into
- last
- let
- letter
- may
- mother
- must
- not
- old
- on
- one
- over
- say
- she
- that
- think
- this
- way
- when
- will
- with

STEP 4—96%
97%
- apple
- bell
- butter
- by
- cook
- door
- eat
- green
- ice
- if
- left
- love
- made
- make
- milk
- night
- said
- school
- six
- snow
- state
- Sunday
- them
- they
- three
- top
- under
- why
- wind
- your

96%
- an
- cake
- cent
- city
- corn
- down
- five
- food
- free
- going
- gold
- hard
- her
- how
- live
- looking
- man
- my
- read
- reader
- red
- sand
- south
- tell
- ten
- we

STEP 5—94%
95%
- about
- after
- age
- ago
- baby
- bank
- bill
- box
- dark
- date
- dinner
- do
- doing
- east
- ever
- face
- foot
- from
- frost
- gave
- had
- hat
- head
- Jan.
- longer
- pay
- place
- pool
- ring
- river
- same
- send
- some
- summer
- sweet
- table
- then
- time
- to-night
- us
- wish
- work
- working

94%
- am
- bad
- bed
- bee
- cannot
- coat
- end
- fast
- faster
- Feb.
- for
- has
- him
- just
- kind
- king
- Monday
- Nov.
- of
- papa
- pig
- play
- real
- ride
- road
- Sat.
- seeing
- silk
- stove
- sun

The Iowa Spelling Scales

till
two
wall
where
wood
yet

STEP 6—92%
93%

along
ask
black
blank
call
child
clean
clock
could
cow
cut
eye
home
hot
however
inside
kiss
lake
life
light
Mr.
much
name
near
never
nice
number
Oct.
off
once
overcoat
playing
price
rich
room
store
thinking
toy
walking
well
who
winter
yard
92%
art
aside
back

ball
below
best
bird
blow
card
cat
clear
cold
cream
cup
far
farm
feet
found
fun
fur
hall
happy
hear
inch
joy
lady
large
lay
lived
lot
March
mark
more
mouth
move
no
note
October
oil
report
rest
saw
small
stage
stand
telling
thanking
told
town
want
week
yellow
91%
air
band
banker
bay
belong
beside
better

blue
came
coal
cover
fat
forget
game
girl
gone
hang
help
house
ink
July
June
keep
kid
looked
lost
low
nine
noon
open
page
park
pen
post
put
rain
reading
sat
sell
sent
show
side
singing
sister
so
sport
standing
stay
stick
supper
there
trip
very
water
while
win
window
yes

STEP 7—88%
90%

any
around

bunch
cap
car
case
country
delay
drive
fellow
fill
fine
gate
goldfish
grade
helping
hill
hog
horse
hour
hunt
late
long
meat
most
next
nut
outside
peach
people
pie
plow
saying
shop
snowed
song
spent
sunshine
take
took
walk
war
wash
went
whatever
wife
without
worker
write
89%
bake
bear
deep
earth
fell
felt
flat
forgot
grass

ground
hen
ill
larger
leave
lunch
new
north
oh
older
part
paying
rock
sheep
sir
snowing
such
taken
teach
test
the
weak
willing
within
word
would
yourself
  88%
able
afternoon
alive
arm
asked
banking
basket
born
bring
can't
care
children
dance
dress
drop
early
even
fall
finding
Friday
grand
handy
here
hold
hunting
landing
law
loved
mad

mail
maker
market
meal
mine
money
mud
now
or
our
pick
pin
rail
rent
rice
row
seat
seen
set
shipment
son
stop
tent
train
trust
  87%
add
added
asking
bat
because
become
being
brand
bright
brother
calling
class
danger
egg
fire
fish
form
glee
lives
luck
meet
morning
myself
net
paper
party
plate
print
sleep
spell
step

sugar
taking
tank
teaching
trunk
wheel

STEP 8—84%
  86%
block
body
cattle
clay
close
count
crop
dad
dandy
December
die
dust
eight
farmer
fishing
flower
gather
hay
heat
holding
inasmuch
master
mill
Miss
neck
nothing
oats
order
outfit
oven
pine
point
porch
pure
quick
railroad
round
sack
seed
sick
smart
space
spot
spring
stamp
starting
still

stood
street
teacher
wild
wishing
  85%
adding
also
barn
bean
boat
camp
colder
dead
deal
don't
feed
first
fort
glass
January
job
know
leg
many
mate
music
nobody
plan
race
reach
recall
rust
sad
saved
seven
shall
short
should
slow
staying
talking
tenth
trying
upon
washing
watch
wheat
wool
  84%
above
battle
been
birthday
bringing
brought
brown

The Iowa Spelling Scales

catch
chair
church
forgive
four
glad
island
kill
kindly
lesson
longest
ma
other
ours
own
pink
pocket
pole
recover
sink
spelling
start
stone
than
too
true
Tuesday
warm
washed
won't
yearly
83%
April
behind
cared
carpet
cash
cooking
cost
counting
dearly
draft
every
farming
father
finger
forest
glove
great
grove
half
harvest
hole
kitten
lump
please
printed

remove
renew
rush
shoe
sixty
someone
sound
speaker
thin
thus
to
were
whenever
wide
82%
agree
anyone
Aug.
aunt
backing
became
blame
bought
boxes
buy
charge
Christmas
died
done
football
given
grandma
grant
gray
hardly
hearing
heating
held
hit
kinder
making
might
moved
paint
pass
passing
person
picking
rate
remark
right
safe
sit
soil
sold
sometime
sort

speak
talk
tip
twenty
unless
used
velvet
wet
white
worked
world

STEP 9—79%

81%
again
ahead
another
belonging
blood
boss
bother
cane
cleaner
clothing
contest
dearest
death
display
doctor
dresser
evening
fifty
fight
ford
hair
harder
having
homesick
inclose
later
lone
noted
patch
post card
renter
rose
shot
sin
soon
sum
swell
these
thick
thought
travel
weather

wonder
yesterday
80%
alone
always
apart
ate
bet
between
Bible
board
both
broke
change
cool
cord
covering
cross
drum
eve
everyone
fair
find
floor
follow
granted
herewith
high
I'm
inches
income
learned
less
listed
liver
load
maid
mailed
mean
nap
none
pa
pain
per
plum
rained
removed
shape
sight
slip
sorry
started
tie
wagon
wake
wanted

wear
young
    79%
asleep
begin
behalf
cleaning
darling
deed
feeding
fence
fit
former
garment
goat
ha
handed
handle
invited
its
jump
leather
mend
pack
queen
raining
rank
riding
self
shut
simple
skate
soap
storm
stranger
teeth
thankful
use
walked
wire
    78%
across
beat
belt
burn
called
cheer
cloth
club
coming
company
dozen
fail
grandfather
hundred
largest
lift

list
lumber
marking
matter
nation
nearly
neat
officer
otherwise
overlooked
pound
printer
proper
roof
sample
sending
seventh
shade
silver
size
somewhere
speed
spending
spoke
stock
sure
Thursday
trade
twice
welcome
wrote
    77%
brick
brush
carry
check
closed
colt
damp
Dec.
file
friend
garden
goose
grain
himself
labor
lace
leader
member
miss
only
pencil
posted
printing
ready
rug

saver
sixth
something
thereafter
thousand
tiny
try
which
whole
worth

STEP 10—73%
    76%
afterward
amount
beg
bench
bite
calf
clever
depend
dream
drew
enough
flour
forth
fresh
gallon
grew
happen
hurt
idea
jar
killed
met
nose
painted
pools
press
pride
program
prove
renting
sash
selling
Sept.
September
steam
their
ticket
tire
unable
understanding
wedding
wise
wishes
woven

    75%
bit
blew
branch
chart
chop
closer
crib
does
dollar
drug
everybody
glasses
heard
holder
I'll
intend
keeping
kindest
liberty
lovely
merry
mighty
month
Mrs.
need
newspaper
office
pair
picture
pillow
proud
provide
rack
rented
rip
rolling
rubber
scout
seem
seventy
shortly
smaller
soft
steel
stunt
team
treat
    74%
act
ans.
anyway
bottle
chance
chicken
cotton
fact

The Iowa Spelling Scales

farther
field
folder
gladly
guess
heavy
herself
joke
kisses
leaves
match
mostly
news
November
ocean
oldest
ordering
phone
post office
quart
rabbit
reached
rule
shame
sis
sock
somewhat
tend
those
tile
together
trace
track
twelve
uncle
understand
voter
west
witch

73%

almost
anything
awhile
building
coffee
county
dread
dressed
easy
enter
everything
failed
front
fruit
grown
heap
inclosed

inspect
iron
likewise
payment
peace
pleased
remain
returned
scrap
seal
spend
study
temple
vote
wanting
whereby

72%

acting
agent
anywhere
army
classes
cleaned
content
dare
deliver
drill
fear
getting
gift
gown
improve
indeed
kindness
maple
o'clock
odd
planted
postage
protest
providing
Pump
roll
seemed
shed
sore
thread
ton
township
turn
wage

71%

answer
ashamed
bid
branches
build

bushel
cast
center
discount
during
eighty
elect
fee
feeling
folk
froze
funny
gain
hate
household
lame
latter
least
living
loaded
mailing
moment
moving
ought
packed
partly
pending
prevent
pull
render
return
rough
saving
sickness
slide
stated
tested
thirty
trusting
visit
wished

70%

anyhow
bog
booklet
coast
copy
corner
depending
enclose
filled
flesh
formed
itself
junk
learn
main

meeting
named
noise
oblige
plain
raised
ranch
reason
repair
rushed
talked
trained
won
wrong
Xmas

STEP 11—66%

69%

afraid
among
Ave.
badly
began
brain
candle
cloudy
court
dated
drilling
family
finish
fourth
French
gee
grind
handling
higher
hoped
kitchen
leaf
mistake
nearer
nicely
nor
orange
past
perfect
range
sale
settle
sewing
snap
strongly
suit
title
withdrew

writer
zone
68%
broad
broken
busy
cause
demand
enjoyed
filling
forward
globe
greater
greeting
growing
health
hers
kept
knew
knowing
known
laugh
letting
perhaps
placing
poorly
powder
raw
respond
Saturday
says
since
stating
strongest
waist
women
worm
67%
already
August
beef
bottom
changed
changing
cottage
dealing
dice
expert
express
few
haven't
helpful
hereafter
housekeeping
including
invite

joined
lighting
locate
lung
meantime
mind
needle
nurse
obliged
payable
plenty
pretty
slipper
third
through
turkey
value
western
wonderful
66%
afloat
all right
beaten
chain
chose
coy
dispose
enjoy
fancy
favor
fifteen
frankly
gas
history
joyful
lie
liked
lucky
membership
nerve
opening
owned
packing
power
proved
provided
remind
spread
stair
that's
throw
vacation
voice
waited
you'll

65%
absent
before
bugs
builder
chairman
cheap
coin
colored
contain
delivered
devoted
dose
frame
fully
gland
grit
handled
highest
hoping
hurry
inviting
learning
leaving
lowest
ordered
painter
parlor
present
produce
retail
serve
share
single
sooner
square
taught
tax
training
understood
weary
64%
breakfast
chapter
closing
earning
extent
extra
fix
freeze
frozen
hotel
inclosing
inform
informed
join
lamb

message
mountain
phoned
picnic
played
prize,
raising
shipping
shoulder
shown
strike
treated
until
valued
weekly
writing
zero
63%
auto
await
checking
delighted
edge
excuse
feeder
figure
finest
fitting
handsome
hare
helped
ivory
mister
monthly
opened
pearl
penny
reaches
regard
sitting
steady
waiting
youth

STEP 12—58%
62%
birth
breaking
chill
chum
contract
cooler
cough
cousin
Dr.
enclosed

The Iowa Spelling Scales

explain
fifth
fitted
forwarding
greatest
hardware
herein
knot
level
manage
painting
quickly
reaching
refuse
rod
score
station
stuff
thereof
to-morrow
wait
workmanship
61%
blessed
charming
cheerful
clearly
dairy
dirty
disposed
duty
extend
friendly
insist
located
loud
lower
piano
reply
sheet
showed
stamped
subject
though
Tues.
visited
worse
60%
adjust
advise
awaiting
Bro.
built
checked
color
comply
direct

ease
improved
intended
invoice
listen
lonesome
loss
mamma
mass
measure
middle
nature
offering
owe
rapid
recovered
repeat
retain
scare
setting
settlement
sew
skating
tread
tried
59%
anybody
appear
capital
caught
covered
crowd
daughter
exchange
fixed
following
force
forwarded
headquarter
hence
limb
loving
manner
namely
pattern
pavement
per cent
performed
placed
proven
quit
quite
record
request
requesting
respect
woman

58%
address
agreed
base
carried
caused
coasting
collar
comfort
cure
damage
delightful
detail
fever
fourteen
guide
habit
illness
I've
ladies
language
linen
lovely
narrow
needing
nineteen
obtain
organ
season
suffering
Thanksgiving
throat
united
voting
57%
answering
beet
beyond
bridge
crazy
crew
deeply
delayed
eager
eighteen
eleventh
finished
further
homestead
honest
husband
latest
lose
married
misses
needed
prevented

profit
public
shock
surprised
taxes
turned
waste
watching
56%
actor
although
baking
boiler
buying
cheaper
confined
contained
daily
dancing
dealer
feel
figured
foolish
furnish
German
happened
I'd
improving
instead
movement
package
quarter
refund
regarding
reported
saddle
sign
slept
tired
useful
Wednesday
whom
55%
amounting
answered
backed
boarding
buggy
bulk
charged
choose
crippled
debate
decline
discovered
enjoying
explained

The Iowa Spelling Scales

fairly
gotten
grip
industry
isn't
lecture
neglect
nevertheless
notice
plainly
pleasure
production
properly
regret
require
suitable
surface
worst

STEP 13—50%

54%
aid
aim
barrel
begun
correct
directed
except
flavor
friendship
gaining
gravy
include
intention
loan
obtained
owing
permit
raise
second
seller
spare
tight
watched
winner
yourselves

53%
adopted
bigger
bowl
buyer
continue
creep
cutting
desire

dodge
fund
future
germ
holiday
insert
ninth
presented
primary
proof
ribbon
scale
struck
supply
suppose
wearing
wouldn't
yoke

52%
abstract
advance
ample
chief
debating
else
entering
fuel
furnishing
headache
hello
item
likely
machine
maybe
model
oversight
passed
perfectly
postal
requested
secure
seldom
stayed
studies
submit
therefore
treatment
trouble
unpaid

51%
action
attend
balance
beauty
coach
daddy

enrolled
excited
film
fullest
graze
investment
length
maintain
outlined
Prof.
property
rainy
remained
remembering
renewed
server
weigh
worry
written

50%
awful
careful
clerk
closely
conduct
entertaining
entry
factory
February
loyal
minute
northern
noticed
pupil
rapidly
served
sleet
standard
statement
truly
using
wondering

49%
advice
alley
ankle
biggest
burden
butcher
captain
consist
containing
delivery
election
example
expressed

forenoon
garage
gentleman
greatly
lbs.
loose
notion
potatoes
promised
queer
quoted
shopping
silence
sorrow
surprise
throughout
trial
upper
valley

48%
adjustment
animal
avenue
aware
break
calm
central
concluded
degree
deportment
dreadful
either
fern
filing
gasoline
hereby
judge
lately
niece
parcel
prospect
putting
recently
recess
recite
returning
settled
skirt
smooth
splendid
stories
taste
topic
traveling
visiting

The Iowa Spelling Scales

47%
addition
admit
aren't
cabinet
cherries
due
fare
lodge.
patent
pleasant
quiet
strict
touch
toward
uniform
whether

46%
account
acted
active
addresses
attending
bass
bluff
booster
button
climate
clothe
credit
enclosing
entered
entertainment
forty
hasn't
honor
increasing
mention
pertaining
progress
promotion
refused
regulation
relationship
rye
satisfied
service
several
sire
student
studying
text
tickled
towel
weighed
we'll

we've
whose
worried
worthy

Step 14—42%

45%
against
artist
companion
considering
couple
exciting
fault
figuring
lining
prompt
question
studied
weight

44%
automobile
booth
carefully
carrying
conversation
destroyed
final
growth
handkerchief
honestly
human
independent
modern
neighborhood
prepaid
problem
replying
required
ruin
serving
shipper
soldier
union

43%
advertised
arrive
average
control
debt
depot
decision
earnest
effort
entirely

ere
explaining
forced
furnace
instant
jobber
jury
mentioned
normal
pardon
parent
popular
rendered
reputation
term
utmost

42%
allow
circus
complete
convention
duties
English
expected
fashion
gentlemen
grocery
included
information
laid
location
recent
shipped
slightly
sweater
view
violin

41%
addressed
apply
blooming
condition
contemplated
dependent
different
drama
dwelling
elected
entertain
extended
famous
favorable
ideal
important
interested
liquid

losing
manufacture
minister
missed
object
parties
piece
preparing
publisher
reduced
refreshment
relation
represent
result
rifle
scarce
situation
worrying

40%
agreeable
barley
blackberries
catalogue
creamery
desired
desiring
expired
gained
healthy
hospital
inquire
local
offered
pastor
preacher
prepare
promptly
realize
reduce
remember
running
struggle
vary

39%
arrange
believe
candidate
carrier
comfortable
common
complaint
constant
director
factor
failure
female

group
haste
installed
ironing
machinery
manager
operated
product
promise
protected
remit
reserve
success
supplied
you'd

38%
advanced
alfalfa
bargain
billed
cement
cigar
confident
convince
curtain
describe
didn't
employed
firm
forgotten
limit
lovingly
manual
method
really
resulting
simply
slippery

STEP 15—34%

37%
ache
acre
argument
attention
choice
current
cute
decide
deserve
discontinued
doesn't
domestic
exact
exactly
feature

hurried
inclined
interest
priced
produced
quote
register
republican
talent
telephone
tract
transit

36%
advantage
adventure
advising
avoid
calves
cellar
considered
couldn't
courage
data
easily
entitle
formerly
furnished
increased
international
Latin
limited
management
owner
prepared
receive
select
supposed
transfer
treasurer

35%
attach
attached
crowded
decided
doubt
expecting
factories
fierce
guest
hadn't
madam
position
prayer
private
represented
resident

respectfully
strawberries

34%
appeal
awfully
capable
certain
cities
college
consider
continued
convinced
deserved
foundation
instruct
instructed
mere
moral
neglected
neighbor
prevail
procured
reduction
reliable
section
separate
source

33%
bracelet
channel
composition
congratulate
customer
democrat
education
enroll
entire
favored
happiness
importance
improvement
library
period
realizing
search
secured
securing
slight
tatting
total
vision

32%
adjusted
advertise
applied
arranged

arrived
braid
district
exam.
general
geography
increase
largely
opera
opinion
positive
published
satisfactory
signed
style
succeeded
themselves
valuable

31%
accomplish
advertising
attain
believing
calendar
combination
constantly
corrected
dangerous
disgusted
followed
graduation
hauled
heir
liberal
million
misunderstanding
neither
ninety
operation
organized
ourselves
personal
raiser
regardless
regular
remedy
selected
stomach
straight
vacant

STEP 16—27%

30%
according
advancement
advised

appointed
appointment
attended
automatic
banquet
cartoon
connected
connecting
copies
corporation
credited
directly
excess
exercise
favorite
federal
funeral
inspector
inst.
moderate
nickel
particular
patron
proceed
publication
reference
reservation
route
suggested
theater
wasn't

29%
accordingly
affair
altogether
ambition
amendment
benefit
cashier
collect
concern
connect
course
etc.
examined
expression
ghost
humor
instance
internal
justified
literary
medicine
planning
refer
system
wholesale

28%
appeared
approved
beginning
Christian
commence
correction
correctly
direction
earliest
exception
hesitate
interesting
nervous
prior
purpose
representation
requirement
safety
strength
submitted
transportation

27%
auntie
based
companies
conference
contrary
democratic
develop
difference
extensive
fortune
gratitude
issue
legal
manufacturing
nephew
president
presume
registration
resource
Sabbath
satisfy
spirit
superintendent
support
telegram

26%
attraction
barely
cedar
coarse
concerning
concert
confirming

deposit
engineering
freight
good-bye
graduating
issued
notify
obligation
personality
prefer
quality
reasonable
relative
remembered
rural
sense
stationary
stopped
supplies

25%
advertisement
author
canned
confer
disposal
doubtless
effect
evidently
influence
inquiry
junior
liable
meant
musical
organize
permanent
purchase
reception
selection
semester
serious
society
strictly
volume

24%
assist
ballot
employer
examine
existing
generous
heretofore
imagine
impossible
justify
national
process

resigned
salesman
secretary
series
suggest
tanning
X-ray

STEP 17—21%
23%
absence
absolute
arriving
article
client
collecting
connection
deliveries
difficulty
engineer
enrollment
experience
frequently
furniture
graduate
grateful
label
occupied
possible
possibly
practicing
purchased
quotation
receiving
registered
salary
subscription
succeed

22%
accent
athletics
business
choir
collection
compelled
consequently
consideration
co-operating
coupon
demonstrated
design
durable
envelope
equipment
explanation
fabric

genuine
hustling
inquires
installment
insurance
investigate
involved
satisfaction
timothy

21%
actual
admission
assured
celebrate
construction
decrease
discourage
establish
established
hastily
investigation
mental
merchandise
patient
policy
practice
qualities
reliability
renewal
sanitary
signature
variety

20%
allowed
assistant
basis
brief
carnival
commerce
confidence
cushion
destination
elsewhere
examiner
identify
instruction
introduction
judgment
legislation
magazine
natural
politics
preparation
receipt
regularly
superior

supervision
surplus
type

19%
appearance
application
arrangement
attempt
choosing
circulation
citizen
considerably
correspond
crochet
difficult
distribution
equally
excitement
expensive
federation
numerous
preliminary
quantity
relieved
straightened
subscriber
sympathy
urge

STEP 18—16%

18%
ability
accident
agriculture
algebra
announce
assembly
assessment
attendance
authorized
certainly
consequence
conservatory
considerable
convenient
council
decision
development
examination
girlie
inferior
institution
introduced
knowledge
meter

planned
probably
relieve
representative
responsible
universal

17%
administrator
conclusion
congratulation
description
disappoint
estimated
excellent
government
inconvenience
indicate
inducement
librarian
notified
operating
presence
proposition
prosperous
readily
received
regretting
terrible
weren't

16%
alumni
arrival
assortment
assure
attractive
available
capacity
circular
crocheting
electrical
entitled
epidemic
evidence
exclusively
fashionable
grammar
individual
invitation
merely
rec'd
remembrance
remittance
successful
supervisor
territory
welfare

15%
agency
allotment
announcement
assignment
assistance
assuring
attorney
electricity
encourage
exceptional
extreme
familiar
generally
geometry
grippe
instructor
instrument
literature
notary
ordinary
possess
practical
previous
profitable
referring
special
surgery
usual

14%
absolutely
additional
auditor
blizzard
completely
consultation
expense
foreign
fundamental
gradually
honorable
mortgage
occasion
quantities
thesis
sincere

STEP 19—12%

13%
applicant
association
assume
canvass
communication
constitution
co-operative

The Iowa Spelling Scales

cordial
demonstration
disagreeable
duplicate
employee
finally
illustrated
impression
necessity
organization
premium
profession
senior
social

12%
acquainted
agricultural
anxious
bulletin
compliment
co-operation
disease
error
executed
exhibit
glorious
majority
merit
naturally
orchestra
similar
university
unusually

11%
acquire
administration
anniversary
confirm
contemplating
correspondent
customary
disappointed
disappointment
enormous
exhausted
favorably
illustrating
immense
material
opportunity
particularly

physical
privilege
recommend
specification
thorough
usually

10%
assurance
bonus
circumstances
commercial
enthusiastic
executive
fraternally
guaranteed
journal
possession
practically
recommendation
response
satisfactorily

Step 20—8%

9%
accompanying
accomplished
activity
advisable
affectionately
annual
approval
assigned
associated
certificate
circuit
equipped
extension
illustration
immediate
leisure
mechanical
principle
substitute

8%
acceptance
accordance
annually
authority
campaign
character
civics

committee
continuous
definite
definitely
fortunate
Hallowe'en
immediately
interfere
occasionally
original
principal
prosperity
tuberculosis
unusual

7%
actually
affidavit
analysis
appreciated
appreciation
commissioner
conveniently
cordially
exhibition
extremely
institute
materially
necessary
official
originally
personally
phosphorus
pneumonia
possibility
referred
soliciting
unnecessary
vicinity
zephyr

Step 21—6%

6%
accommodate
acknowledge
ambitious
appreciate
candidacy
confirmation
correspondence
enthusiasm
especially

guarantee
maturity
responsibility

5%
accredited
attitude
convenience
courteous
efficient
essential
exceptionally
physician
professional
science
specially
sufficient
various

Step 22—4%

4%
acquaintance
appreciating
associate
chautauqua
commission
community
financial
ingredients
license
rheumatism
solicit
thoroughly

3%
anticipating
bureau
efficiency
lieutenant
politician
schedule
sincerely

Step 23—2%
appendicitis

Step 24—1%
anticipate
apparatus
peculiarities
scientific

Step 25—0%
characteristic

SECTION XII

THE IOWA SPELLING SCALE

GRADE V

GRADE V

Step 1—100%

all
and
at
baby
book
but
come
day
good
got
hand
have
he
her
his
how
is
it
let
lot
may
old
read
run
say
see
this
three
up
we
what
will
wish
with
wood
year
your

Step 2—99%

age
are
ball
barn
be
big
boy
by
call
came
can
card
corn
could
dear
did
dinner
door
dress
each
every
fast
fish
five
game
go
going
happy
hard
home
hunt
in
July
kind
lake
land
last
letter
like
little
long
look
love
make
man
May
Monday
mother
must
my
not
Nov.
on
out
over
place
play
rich
said
seven
she
ship
snow
state
tell
thank
that
thing
think
top
under
was
way
winter
work

Step 3—98%

add
am
away
bank
bell
bill
box
bring
cake
calling
car
care
cash
clear
dark
do
dog
east
feet
food
foot
from
gate
gold
had
hay
head
help
however
ice
if
inside
into
just
day
men
much
nine
oil
one
park
saw
saying
school
show
silk
so
south
spend
spring
store
taken
ten
the
them
then
train
walking
wall
why
would
yet
yourself

Step 4—96% 97%

about
after
ago
along
apple
asking
back
bed
bee
blow
brother
butter
city
class
clean
count
cow
cut
dance
date
down
earth
end
fall
farm
fat

The Iowa Spelling Scales

fell	time	half	working
fire	to-day	hall	yard
free	to-night	heat	
gave	two	hen	STEP 5—94%
get	us	hill	*95%*
give	very	hold	
grade	walk	inch	added
has	wash	joy	afternoon
hat	well	king	art
hot	whatever	large	asked
ill	where	late	backing
ink	white	lost	banking
June	who	mail	bay
kindly	within	market	bean
left	world	mean	below
light	you	mill	beside
live	*96%*	move	black
longer	adding	note	blank
looking	an	number	boat
made	as	our	brick
milk	bad	pine	cannot
more	became	point	change
most	best	poor	coal
Mr.	better	print	cream
night	bird	rain	cup
north	block	reader	dead
nut	blue	reading	Dec.
off	bright	real	eat
once	cap	road	Feb.
outside	case	same	felt
Page	cat	sell	filling
papa	cent	short	finding
pay	chair	side	Friday
pig	children	sister	frost
put	coat	spell	girl
red	cold	spelling	glass
rent	cook	standing	grass
river	cover	stone	ground
rush	covering	summer	grove
sand	dad	Sunday	handy
seen	delay	table	him
send	doing	thanking	hog
sheep	dust	there	hour
should	early	till	house
sick	ever	toy	hunting
six	face	tree	Jan.
some	farming	used	kid
stand	faster	want	landing
stay	fellow	war	law
such	fill	washing	lived
sun	for	water	low
sweet	found	went	mad
take	fun	west	March
tent	glad	wheat	meat
they	goldfish	when	morning
thinking	grand	wide	mud
	green	window	myself

The Iowa Spelling Scales

name
near
net
never
nice
of
oldest
paper
part
pen
picture
playing
price
ready
rest
rice
ride
rock
Sat.
sent
shoe
singing
sink
sleep
sound
start
storm
stove
teacher
telling
thin
took
unable
were
wind
wise
without
worker

94%

able
above
ahead
air
also
arm
around
ask
banker
bat
bear
because
behind
belong
contest
cost
country

cross
darling
deep
died
don't
drive
even
eye
far
fight
first
fishing
fit
forget
glove
gone
great
keep
kiss
lady
larger
leader
leave
leg
life
longest
looked
ma
meal
mine
no
now
Oct.
older
open
or
overcoat
party
pick
pie
pin
proper
rail
reach
remove
report
room
rose
round
rust
sad
safe
sat
shall
sin
slip

slow
son
song
soon
sport
stamp
stated
stick
stop
swell
teaching
teeth
ticket
trip
upon
wake
warm
wife
willing
worked
yellow
yes

STEP 6—92%
93%

act
alone
any
anyone
aside
bake
become
belt
board
body
boxes
camp
can't
child
colder
cool
crop
done
eight
father
flat
fort
four
goat
hair
handed
handle
hear
himself
inches
lesson

list
liver
lives
load
loved
luck
mark
master
mate
money
mouth
new
noon
nothing
oats
oh
painted
pass
post
postage
press
quick
rule
sack
saved
seed
seeing
sending
set
seventy
silver
sir
sit
small
soft
soil
spending
spent
stage
started
staying
still
stood
sugar
supper
teach
test
town
walked
week
whenever
while
yearly
zone
92%
another
April

The Iowa Spelling Scales 81

army	sold	paint	flower
ate	spot	Pump	garden
basket	talking	queen	gift
birthday	these	rubber	glasses
cattle	told	snowed	growing
check	trust	soap	hang
cleaning	twenty	something	harder
clock	western	sorry	harvest
close		speak	here
December	*91%*	sum	hit
die	alive	sunshine	holding
drop	aunt	taking	income
easily	band	talk	itself
egg	beat	tenth	kindness
fence	been	than	kitten
fine	being	tip	know
forgot	branch	tire	lace
form	bringing	ton	listed
fur	buy	true	lump
grant	cane	trunk	marking
heating	charge	try	nation
helping	chart	Tuesday	nearly
job	church	unless	neck
jump	clay	wanted	none
kill	coffee	wanting	noted
kinder	danger	washed	November
lumber	deal	welcome	office
next	deed	wheel	ours
only	depend	win	outfit
other	dream	wire	person
pack	enough	wishing	pure
packing	feed	wonder	range
paying	fifty	write	rank
people	friend		rate
picking	given		recover
pillow	ha	STEP 7—88%	remain
pink	hardly		remark
planted	heavy	*90%*	rented
plate	high	Aug.	retain
please	hole	blood	return
plow	homesick	both	shame
pocket	horse	brought	shape
pound	January	brush	sort
pride	keeping	bunch	space
printed	lame	burn	station
railroad	largest	called	steam
recall	lunch	catch	study
renter	mailed	chum	tank
seat	matter	classes	thereafter
self	meet	club	those
September	mostly	content	thus
shipment	moved	county	trained
shop	music	dearest	use
sickness	nobody	dresser	wagon
smart	order	farmer	wet
snowing	oven	fear	wild
	own	file	

wool
word
worth
yesterday

89%

acting
booklet
born
bottle
bought
brain
brand
cared
carry
center
chop
closed
coast
cooking
dated
discount
display
dollar
dozen
drug
drum
duty
everything
express
fact
fail
few
filled
gather
getting
happen
hate
hurry
invite
leaves
less
maid
mailing
maker
many
might
news
painter
partly
patch
peach
phone
plenty
pole
post card
printing

protest
pull
race
rained
render
roof
row
settle
shortly
shut
sixty
size
speaker
stranger
street
strongest
suit
sure
temple
thick
travel
trying
understand
watch
weak
woven
young

88%

agree
bet
blame
cheer
Christmas
closer
cord
counting
enter
evening
everyone
fair
finish
follow
football
force
forest
former
front
funny
garment
grain
gray
grown
holder
hoped
I'm
indeed

lift
lovely
membership
met
newspaper
nose
October
passing
per
plan
raw
right
ring
sale
saving
selling
Sept.
skate
snap
spoke
starting
step
stunt
team
thankful
thought
tie
township
track
turkey
uncle
understanding
united
vote
wrote

87%

across
again
agent
always
apart
asleep
awhile
Bible
boss
bother
build
calf
charming
chicken
cloth
coin
crib
dandy
family
feeling

finger
ford
forgive
frame
goose
grandma
grew
hearing
herself
inasmuch
learned
learning
leaving
Miss
miss
month
noise
orange
otherwise
pleased
posted
prevent
printer
quart
raised
removed
respect
roll
seventh
share
shot
sight
someone
somewhere
stock
tend
tile
title
trace
treat
trusting

STEP 8—84%

86%

almost
amount
answer
anything
begin
behalf
bid
bite
cleaner
coasting
cotton
death

The Iowa Spelling Scales

deliver
demand
doctor
draft
eve
exchange
failed
figure
finished
gown
grandfather
hardware
held
history
improve
knew
learn
making
match
moving
named
need
pain
peace
pending
poorly
power
rack
raining
reaching
renew
renting
rug
sample
scout
sock
tested
thereof
thread
too
twice
value
velvet
wear
won

85%
absent
anywhere
belonging
building
carpet
cast
cause
caused
chance
contain
cottage

court
damp
dare
dearly
depending
dressed
drew
drill
edge
greatest
grind
heap
honest
household
inform
invited
island
killed
kisses
labor
leather
locate
lower
nature
overlooked
pa
painting
pair
plum
porch
present
reported
riding
rolling
Saturday
seem
sometime
third
thousand
Thursday
treated
turn
waited
whole
wishes
withdraw

84%
afraid
August
auto
battle
bench
between
branches
brown
bushel
chill

clothing
cloudy
company
dispose
does
enjoy
fancy
feeding
folder
forth
frankly
fresh
glee
having
heard
higher
hundred
I'll
improved
inclosed
iron
joke
least
loaded
lone
lonesome
loud
lung
meantime
member
merry
mighty
monthly
nap
nicely
produce
proud
provide
raise
record
repair
request
rod
shade
sheet
showed
simple
since
smaller
somewhat
stair
strongly
taxes
their
tried
weather
wished

83%
active
address
ans.
badly
beet
beg
bit
broken
bugs
builder
candle
changed
clever
colt
conduct
copy
drilling
eighteen
excuse
extent
field
formed
gladly
hereafter
hotel
inclose
lighting
located
lucky
maple
meeting
middle
northern
offering
packed
payment
pearl
plain
prize
ranch
respond
returned
rough
scale
second
single
sixth
slipper
sooner
thirty
to
treatment
vacation
visit
witch
won't

writing
youth
zero

82%

action
afterward
already
among
boiler
broad
broke
cleaned
cure
decline
delighted
eighty
elect
everybody
flesh
floor
froze
fruit
gaining
globe
granted
herewith
instead
joyful
kindest
lamb
leaf
liberty
lie
living
mountain
Mrs.
neat
obtain
ocean
officer
pencil
pretty
program
prove
proved
provided
question
requested
rip
rushed
scare
several
stuff
throat
through
tiny

twelve
understood
voter
waiting
weary
wedding
whereby
women
wonderful
yoke

STEP 9—79%

81%

advance
anyhow
blew
button
buyer
caught
central
chain
clearly
damage
daughter
degree
enclosed
find
finest
flour
folk
fuel
gallon
greeting
haven't
helped
hence
later
laugh
mind
mister
nearer
nor
opening
outlined
payable
phoned
played
prevented
production
quickly
reduce
refuse
retail
seal
seemed

setting
spread
square
steel
subject
talked
tread
valley
voice
waist
which
worm

80%

afloat
anyway
artist
breakfast
bridge
cheap
corner
cutting
delivered
directed
English
fixed
greater
greatly
health
hers
hurt
junk
likewise
mass
mend
needed
needle
nevertheless
notice
o'clock
ordering
pools
post office
potatoes
raising
repeat
sew
shed
strike
studies
though
trade

79%

amounting
before
bottom
carried

charged
climate
comfort
comply
cousin
dealer
dealing
deeply
deserve
dose
expert
extend
feeder
fifth
foolish
frozen
germ
guess
homestead
informed
judge
listen
main
moment
obtained
Penny
postal
power
product
public
reached
reason
recovered
remind
season
serve
speed
stamped
student
suitable
throw
trouble
turned
union
upper
valued
visited
wait
whom
wrong

78%

answering
beef
chapter
crazy
daily

The Iowa Spelling Scales

dancing
dread
election
factory
farther
fix
fourth
fully
gas
German
grit
handling
idea
inspect
isn't
jar
kitchen
knowing
language
latest
latter
liked
message
package
perhaps
reply
returning
sash
score
skating
slide
steady
that's
tired
visiting
we'll
worse

77%

acted
blessed
busy
cheerful
coming
contract
couple
direct
eleventh
enclose
excited
explain
extra
fashion
favor
gain
habit
handsome

herein
insist
intend
joined
lbs.
now
nerve
nurse
odd
opened
ought
past
placed
pleasure
proven
rabbit
require
tax
weekly
weigh
weight
woman
Xmas.

STEP 10—73%

76%

abstract
answered
bigger
built
bulk
capital
cheaper
checked
clerk
cough
dairy
detail
dodge
eager
else
figured
freeze
furnish
grip
headache
housekeeping
intended
join
kept
lecture
loving
machine
married
mistake

movement
perfect
permit
plainly
primary
reaches
scrap
sis
training
truly
until
watching

75%

although
animal
appear
ashamed
Ave.
beaten
begun
birth
changing
checking
coach
creep
ease
factor
forty
fourteen
friendly
gained
gland
helpful
its
level
linen
manage
notion
object
ordered
organ
owing
parlor
providing
ribbon
slept
sorrow
stating
term
together
touch
useful
view
worst
writer

74%

acre
actor
anybody
attend
backed
barrel
beauty
beyond
buying
captain
color
coy
enclosing
except
explained
further
gee
handled
highest
improving
inviting
ivory
known
length
local
measure
million
misses
needing
owner
picnic
profit
rapid
recite
relation
relationship
section
secure
silence
skirt
soldier
sore
statement
taught
throughout
to-morrow
towel
unpaid

73%

agreed
await
chairman
closing
collar
cooler

covered
deportment
disposed
dreadful
during
enjoyed
expected
famous
French
furnished
gasoline
hare
healthy
including
investment
letting
lodge
lonely
oblige
perfectly
piano
property
prospect
quarter
regulation
saddle
saver
settlement
shock
submit
Thanksgiving
traveling
voting

72%
apply
baking
base
bog
careful
cigar
correct
crowd
curtain
devoted
discovered
dwelling
earning
elected
enjoying
entering
feel
fever
fifteen
film
flavor
forward

holiday
hospital
inclosing
include
intention
invoice
ladies
namely
owe
parties
per cent
promised
putting
quit
recess
reduction
regard
reserve
sewing
shipping
shoulder
stayed
supply
uniform
wage

71%
addresses
advise
alley
barley
began
break
carrier
cities
containing
continue
delayed
desired
dice
dirty
fitting
foundation
furnishing
gentleman
handkerchief
hoping
human
husband
illness
increasing
knot
likely
limb
loyal
owned
pavement
pupil

rainy
remember
says
serving
sleet
suffering
Tues.
winner
workmanship

70%
admit
advice
awaiting
blooming
bluff
booth
buggy
butcher
delightful
desire
earnest
explaining
fullest
furnace
graze
happened
loss
model
neglect
nineteen
parent
placing
presented
problem
progress
quoted
reduced
rye
scarce
seller
served
server
spare
sweater
Wednesday
we've
wouldn't
you'll

STEP 11—66%

69%
according
aid
balance
calm
cement

couldn't
delivery
director
district
doubt
Dr.
example
expressed
fitted
fortune
forwarding
geography
grocery
headquarter
important
improvement
insert
I've
lowest
manner
minute
normal
obliged
quite
recently
refreshment
refused
sign
sitting
surface
topic
waste
watched
worry
yourselves

68%
adjust
advising
ample
aware
believe
chose
common
condition
consist
contained
credit
employed
fairly
forenoon
forgotten
friendship
fund
hurried
I'd
inquire

The Iowa Spelling Scales

jury
location
performed
prepaid
properly
requesting
result
settled
shown
stories
struck
success
wasn't

67%

adjustment
boarding
circus
companion
dangerous
fault
fern
figuring
forwarded
included
information
ironing
method
promise
recent
regret
remained
simply
standard
wondering

66%

account
addressed
attending
breaking
burden
colored
debate
dependent
expecting
February
ideal
industry
maybe
modern
neighbor
noticed
passed
pertaining
private
protected
queer

rapidly
remembering
renewed
seldom
suppose
utmost
written

65%

ache
aim
attention
closely
convention
current
debating
due
education
entirely
entry
fare
hadn't
instruction
item
loan
neglected
pattern
preparing
prompt
promptly
running
search
select
text
tickled
tight
wearing
weighed

64%

allow
arrive
avenue
average
bowl
cherries
chief
collect
crippled
domestic
entitle
fee
hereby
interested
minister
offered
ourselves
prepare

produced
required
shipper
smooth
surprise
taste
therefore
toward
tract
using
worthy

63%

addition
against
ankle
complaint
constant
depot
didn't
direction
directly
entered
entertainment
exciting
following
general
gentlemen
gotten
group
hasn't
hello
honor
interest
period
prayer
replying
separate
struggle
tanning
violin

STEP 12—58%

62%

ability
advanced
avoid
blackberries
carefully
creamery
daddy
describe
duties
entertain
entire
favorable

followed
guide
independent
lately
lining
management
moral
oversight
parcel
piece
proceed
proof
regular
remit
rifle
strict
surprised
total
trial
you'd

61%

advised
automobile
biggest
calves
choice
concluded
conversation
cute
decide
deposit
deserved
difference
final
musical
ninth
preacher
promotion
quality
quiet
regarding
whose

60%

advantage
adventure
argument
Bro.
comfortable
complete
confined
consider
continued
debt
extended
factories
future

ghost
gravy
inspector
instant
interesting
limit
lose
madam
mamma
national
published
reputation
shopping
sire
slightly
studied
vision

59%

alfalfa
channel
connected
contemplated
decided
destroyed
different
excess
feature
firm
funeral
laid
liberal
maintain
mention
natural
notify
operation
pardon
position
presume
procured
remembered
republican
ruin
satisfied
service
style
supplied
usual
whether

58%

appeal
appeared
aren't
braid
cabinet

capable
clothe
connecting
contrary
control
correctly
doubtless
either
enrolled
entertaining
favored
forced
garage
growth
honestly
loose
lovingly
machinery
manufacture
mentioned
misunderstanding
patent
pleasant
prepared
priced
register
represent
telephone
theatre
volume

57%

adjusted
author
billed
cellar
confer
division
drama
federal
filing
installed
manager
nephew
pastor
president
prevail
publication
secured
signed
transfer
transportation

56%

appointed
arrange

assure
cedar
choose
considering
convince
courage
crew
enroll
exact
expired
freight
furniture
graduating
guest
impossible
instructed
junior
manufacturing
operated
popular
purchase
refer
selection
slight
studying
supplies
vacant
worried

55%

accept
advancement
advertise
agreeable
attended
bass
collecting
commence
concert
constantly
effort
failure
female
inclined
instruct
liable
limited
missed
publisher
rendered
series
shipped
special
transit
treasurer
valuable

STEP 13—50%

54%

affair
awful
considered
corrected
correction
credited
doesn't
effect
generous
hesitate
internal
library
liquid
losing
neighborhood
neither
particular
possible
purpose
receive
refund
reliable
represented
requirement
resident
resulting
route
salesman
selected

53%

advertised
article
assist
automatic
carrying
concerning
consideration
course
humor
increase
jobber
largely
nickel
patient
Prof.
quotation
reference
serious
stomach
straight
support
supposed
worrying

The Iowa Spelling Scales

52%
actual
cashier
catalogue
certain
crowded
discourage
disgusted
earliest
exactly
exam.
federation
formerly
graduation
increased
introduction
medicine
operating
opinion
personal
practice
reasonable
regardless
slippery
telegram

51%
absence
adopted
bracelet
calendar
college
confidence
connect
copies
desiring
discontinued
durable
employer
encourage
expression
imagine
realize
safety
spirit
strawberries
subscriber
weren't

50%
arrived
bargain
commerce
construction
deliveries
easily
extensive
graduate

hauled
justified
manual
niece
really
satisfaction
situation
stationary

49%
arrival
benefit
certainly
coarse
confident
convinced
enrollment
exception
favorite
instance
involved
literary
occupied
opera
organized
positive
remedy
satisfactory
splendid
succeed
system
vary

48%
applied
attempt
believing
circular
composition
connection
considerable
democrat
democratic
good-bye
haste
importance
numerous
patron
raiser
respectfully
responsible
strength
wholesale

47%
accomplish
announce
attached
attain

beginning
booster
fierce
hustling
investigation
Latin
moderate
personality
prefer
rural
strictly
tatting

46%
advertising
all right
attach
banquet
compelled
cushion
data
decrease
difficulty
envelope
establish
expensive
fashionable
happiness
nervous
ninety
process
relative
sanitary
society
source
succeeded
talent
terrible
type

Step 14—42%

45%
absolute
altogether
amendment
approved
assured
cartoon
choosing
Christian
concern
conclusion
develop
equally
exercise
inducement

label
notified
quote
securing
themselves

44%
arriving
attraction
circulation
conference
customer
elsewhere
fortunate
frequently
honorable
meant
mere
obligation
policy
purchased
reception
reservation
suggest

43%
accident
brief
celebrate
citizen
combination
established
glorious
grammar
influence
issue
planned
practical
profitable
realizing
relieved
timothy
universal

42%
auntie
available
canned
collection
congratulate
destination
difficult
electrical
ere
examine
government
gratitude
heretofore

introduced
invitation
justify
knowledge
mental
previous
qualities
receiving
regularly
resigned
salary
stopped
university
41%
allowed
companies
explanation
grateful
indicate
instructor
insurance
international
profession
sincere
40%
anxious
assortment
awfully
blizzard
business
candidate
congratulation
contemplating
etc.
generally
identify
investigate
legal
Possibly
readily
relieve
satisfy
sense
suggested
surplus
territory
39%
agriculture
ambition
appointment
assembly
attractive
choir
confirming
co-operating
corporation

disease
estimated
examined
impression
received
representation
social
submitted
superintendent
38%
barely
considerably
design
equipment
expense
experience
instrument
material
registered
renewal
Sabbath
semester
signature
subscription
superior
urge

Step 15—34%
37%
application
authorized
coupon
description
development
disagreeable
disposal
engineer
entitled
error
majority
merchandise
proposition
successful
36%
advertisement
agency
arranged
confirm
disappoint
evidence
favorably
genuine
merely
organize

supervision
welfare
35%
appreciate
assurance
ballot
basis
distribution
engineering
heir
prosperous
quantity
34%
assistant
fabric
illustration
installment
merit
rec'd
reliability
variety
33%
activity
based
canvass
conservatory
co-operative
crochet
demonstrated
electricity
excitement
hastily
literature
meter
notary
presence
prior
registration
secretary
sympathy
32%
attendance
client
compliment
consequently
consultation
duplicate
employee
examination
inst.
issued
ordinary
planning
practicing
preliminary

resource
supervisor
31%
absolutely
accordingly
assistance
auditor
commercial
council
existing
foreign
magazine
politics
various
vicinity

Step 16—27%
30%
administration
advisable
allotment
announcement
circumstances
crocheting
demonstration
exceptional
executed
illustrated
inquiry
journal
organization
principal
principle
remembrance
similar
29%
acquire
actually
assuring
athletics
enormous
fundamental
girlie
institute
naturally
possess
response
straightened
thesis
unusual
28%
acquainted
arrangement
assignment
completely
convenient

The Iowa Spelling Scales

co-operation
examiner
excellent
extreme
finally
gradually
orchestra
particularly
permanent
preparation
quantities
senior
substitute
X-ray

27%
additional
administrator
admission
applicant
civics
commission
consequence
evidently
inquires
institution
premium
receipt
satisfactorily
usually

26%
algebra
appearance
assume
correspond
immense
judgment
official
physician
probably
thorough

25%
attitude
carnival
constitution
continuous
customary
disappointed
equipped
individual
occasionally
original
possibility

24%
alumni
approval
bulletin

confirmation
cordially
decision
disappointment
epidemic
exhibit
familiar
geometry
illustrating
interfere
sincerely

STEP 17—21%
23%
acquaintance
annual
annually
association
essential
exclusively
exhausted
grippe
maturity
necessary
opportunity
remittance
representative
unusually

22%
assigned
certificate
character
communication
enthusiastic
librarian
personally
privilege
regretting
science
surgery

21%
assessment
especially
extremely
inferior
mechanical
prosperity
responsibility

20%
acceptance
accordance
agricultural
associated
attorney
circuit

mortgage
occasion
physical
solicit

19%
accompanying
bonus
campaign
cordial
correspondent
executive
license
professional
specification

STEP 18—16%
18%
appreciating
bureau
convenience
exceptionally
extension
Hallowe'en
legislation
necessity
pneumonia

17%
accomplished
affidavit
appreciation
commissioner
community
inconvenience
originally
practically
recommend
referred
scientific
unnecessary

16%
candidacy
capacity
efficient
exhibition
financial
guaranteed
immediately
leisure
sufficient

15%
acknowledge
anticipate
correspondence
fraternally
referring

14%
analysis
appreciated
enthusiasm
immediate
possession——
tuberculosis

STEP 19—12%
13%
accredited
apparatus
authority
thoroughly
12%
accommodate
associate
courteous
peculiarities
phosphorus
11%
affectionately
ambitious
politician
specially
10%
anniversary
conveniently
recommendation

STEP 20—8%
9%
definite
ingredients
materially
8%
chautauqua
committee
definitely
zephyr
7%
anticipating
guarantee
rheumatism
soliciting

STEP 21—6%
6%
efficiency
lieutenant
5%
appendicitis
schedule

STEP 22—4%
4%
characteristic

SECTION XIII

THE IOWA SPELLING SCALE

GRADE VI

GRADE VI

Step 1—100%

age
and
as
away
best
big
bill
book
boy
but
call
can
care
clear
cover
dear
did
dog
door
dress
each
end
ever
fast
father
feet
found
from
get
give
go
gold
good
grand
happy
has
he
helping
his
hog
home
how
if
is
it
just
lake
large
larger
let
live
long
may
me
more
most
must
my
name
old
on
one
out
over
place
put
read
reader
real
rest
run
said
same
say
see
she
should
stand
tell
thank
that
the
them
they
thing
this
train
tree
under
walk
walked
was
way
we
went
what
when
will
wish
with
working
year

Step 2—99%

able
about
add
all
along
am
an
apple
are
at
back
bad
ball
bank
be
bell
better
bird
black
blank
blow
box
butter
check
child
city
clean
coat
cold
come
cook
corn
could
day
deal
dinner
do
doing
down
eat
even
face
farm
farming
faster
fat
fire
fish
five
food
girl
got
grass
green
hard
have
head
help
hold
holding
ice
in
inside
into
July
land
last
lay
letter
light
like
little
lot
love
made
make
man
May
milk
Monday
move
much
myself
never
not
nut
oil
other
park
pay
peach
play
rain
rich
ride
ring
rock
rust
saying
school
sell
send
seven
ship

The Iowa Spelling Scales

show	battle	however	sand
singing	because	hunt	saw
small	bee	ill	seed
snow	brand	ink	seeing
so	bring	Jan.	shall
soil	brother	June	sheep
some	bunch	keep	sick
spell	by	kind	sickness
sport	cake	labor	silk
state	came	lady	slow
stay	cannot	late	soon
stone	car	law	south
table	card	life	spelling
take	case	lived	spend
taken	changed	longer	spot
ten	class	look	spring
test	clock	looking	standing
thanking	close	lost	start
think	contest	loved	stop
three	country	mark	store
till	covering	market	stove
time	cow	master	such
top	cross	meal	summer
understanding	cut	mill	sweet
up	dark	mine	swell
us	date	money	talking
very	Dec.	mother	thinking
wagon	December	nation	to-day
washing	delay	near	ton
well	early	next	trip
west	eight	night	Tuesday
wheat	every	nine	two
while	eye	noon	unless
who	fail	note	used
why	fall	Nov.	wall
wide	fill	of	want
window	foot	off	wanting
without	for	once	week
wood	four	outside	white
work	free	page	wife
worked	Friday	paper	wild
would	game	part	wishing
yet	gave	pick	within
you	going	please	worker
your	grade	point	yard
	had	poor	yellow
STEP 3—98%	hand	post	yes
	hat	print	yourself
after	hay	reach	zone
ago	heat	red	
air	her	remove	STEP 4—96%
arm	hill	rent	97%
around	him	report	
art	homesick	river	above
ask	hot	room	adding
bake	hour	rush	again
barn	house	sample	agree

alone	fur	renter	bottle
any	glad	rice	bought
asked	glass	Sat.	boxes
baby	gone	sat	braid
backing	growing	sent	burn
band	half	set	buy
banker	handy	shoe	called
banking	harder	sink	cap
basket	harvest	sister	cash
bat	held	six	cattle
bed	here	size	charge
being	high	sleep	charming
below	holder	snowed	children
beside	horse	soap	clay
birthday	hundred	sound	coast
blue	hunting	space	cool
body	joy	stick	cost
bother	killed	sum	cotton
branch	kindly	sun	dandy
bringing	kindness	talk	depend
building	landing	tank	dressed
bushel	leader	teaching	drive
calling	left	then	dust
cat	looked	thin	earning
cent	low	to-night	enter
chair	luck	took	farmer
change	ma	town	few
Christmas	mad	treat	figure
clothing	mail	try	first
coal	maker	unable	flower
coin	meat	walking	forget
count	morning	wash	fort
counting	Mr.	water	friend
crop	net	whatever	fruit
dance	north	where	garment
danger	number	wind	gate
deep	office	winter	gather
display	only	wire	gift
dollar	our	write	given
done	oven	yearly	glasses
drop	overcoat	*96%*	grain
earth	pack	added	great
east	party	ahead	ground
edge	people	alive	hang
far	per	also	hate
feed	picture	another	himself
fell	pig	anyone	hit
fellow	pin	asking	inch
felt	pine	become	inches
fifty	plate	behind	income
fight	playing	belonging	jump
finding	pound	belt	kid
fishing	price	block	kinder
forgot	proper	blood	king
form	rail	board	learn
fun	reading	boat	leave
	ready	boss	leg

96 *The Iowa Spelling Scales*

The Iowa Spelling Scales

lesson	slip	degree	rented
lift	smart	delighted	renting
listed	soft	died	rolling
longest	sold	draft	rose
lunch	song	dream	rule
mailed	spent	drew	seat
March	spoke	eighty	seem
marking	stamp	enough	seen
mouth	started	evening	self
mud	stated	Feb.	selling
music	station	fence	Sept.
newspaper	study	filling	shame
nice	sunshine	follow	shipment
no	Sunday	forgive	side
nothing	supper	former	sin
ocean	teacher	frost	snowing
Oct.	telling	glove	son
October	tent	goat	sort
older	than	goose	spending
oldest	third	grove	step
or	track	handle	stood
order	trained	hear	stump
outfit	trunk	heating	sugar
paint	war	hereafter	taking
papa	were	inspect	teach
paying	whenever	job	teeth
payment	willing	kill	tenth
person	wise	kiss	tested
phone	wool	learned	thereafter
pink	word	leather	these
pleased	worth	liver	thick
printed		maple	thousand
provide		mate	ticket
pure	Step 5—94%	mean	tire
quart	*95%*	meet	told
raised		meeting	trace
rate	act	mend	true
reached	bay	moved	trust
remain	bet	new	trusting
remark	blame	now	twice
request	booklet	obtain	understood
return	born	oh	value
road	brick	open	wake
roof	bridge	otherwise	watch
row	brush	own	win
sack	calf	painted	world
sad	camp	passing	young
saved	carpet	pen	
sending	chicken	pie	*94%*
settle	cities	plain	advance
sheet	club	pole	afternoon
shop	company	press	always
short	cord	Pump	amount
shut	cup	quick	army
simple	dad	range	aunt
sir	darling	rank	auto
sixty	dead	recover	beat
	dearly		become

The Iowa Spelling Scales

been	offering	awhile	many
between	pain	bear	matter
bright	partly	began	member
brought	pass	bench	might
build	payable	branches	mighty
catch	pending	broken	nature
center	pillow	chain	nerve
chart	post card	chop	nicely
cleaning	power	church	nose
cloth	pride	cleaned	overlooked
coffee	pull	closed	pa
contract	railroad	colder	packing
cooking	rained	content	painting
crib	recall	copy	pair
dare	removed	correct	plenty
dealing	reported	cottage	pocket
depending	round	court	postage
discount	rushed	cream	prevent
doctor	scout	cure	printer
egg	season	damage	protest
English	seventh	daughter	ranch
enjoy	seventy	dearest	reaching
feeding	silver	death	repair
file	skate	deed	respect
finish	something	don't	retain
finished	sometime	dresser	rod
fit	somewhat	drug	rubber
flat	sorry	drum	September
funny	speak	easy	serve
garden	stage	enclose	share
getting	steam	everybody	shortly
gladly	still	exchange	showed
goldfish	street	fact	sit
grant	strongest	farther	slipper
granted	subject	fine	smaller
greater	thankful	folder	somewhere
hall	those	folk	sooner
hardly	thread	fully	speaker
heap	trying	gain	starting
heavy	twenty	gallon	staying
hen	upon	ha	stranger
January	vacation	hair	tend
joyful	vote	handed	there
kitchen	weather	happen	Thursday
kitten	western	hearing	tip
know	wet	herewith	training
lame	whereby	history	twelve
least	wrote	indeed	union
list		island	united
load	Step 6—92%	jar	valued
locate	*93%*	leaves	weak
lower		liberty	wedding
lump	agent	likewise	welcome
match	answer	loaded	withdraw
nearly	anything	located	yesterday
noise	asleep	lone	
oats	ate	lovely	

The Iowa Spelling Scales

92%

address
already
appear
April
aside
August
author
bean
before
belong
bite
both
broke
busy
cane
can't
carry
cast
caused
charged
checking
chum
classes
contain
cooler
county
damp
dated
does
dozen
drill
duty
expert
express
family
fancy
filled
flesh
fresh
friendly
front
grandfather
grandma
gray
higher
honest
hurt
instead
invited
iron
itself
join
joined
keeping
kisses
lace

largest
learning
less
living
loyal
merry
moment
mostly
named
nearer
neck
need
nobody
officer
ordering
patch
planted
present
printing
production
proved
public
queen
reason
renew
returned
safe
shed
shot
sixth
square
strongly
studies
trade
uncle
use
visit
waited
waiting
wanted
wheel
which
wished
wonder
wrong
zero

91%

active
among
answered
anybody
beg
behalf
Bible
broad
chance
chapter

cleaner
closer
cloudy
cutting
delightful
demand
desire
elect
eve
everyone
everything
extend
extra
fear
feeling
fixed
forest
freeze
French
froze
frozen
gained
greeting
grown
having
hence
herself
hole
including
ivory
joke
judge
knowing
leaving
listen
lives
location
mailing
membership
mind
Miss
news
none
normal
package
plow
pools
postal
product
program
provided
race
raise
reduce
remind
render
reply

requested
requesting
require
respond
rug
sale
saving
scale
second
snap
stock
taught
tax
team
their
thought
tile
title
to
treated
understood
washed
wear
whole

STEP 7—88%

90%

acting
aim
almost
ashamed
Aug.
beef
bid
builder
changing
cheap
cheaper
coasting
conduct
contained
continue
corner
daily
deeply
die
direct
dispose
dread
ease
enjoyed
excuse
extent
factory
failed
fair

favor
flavor
floor
formed
frame
fuel
gaining
grind
grit
heard
hoped
I'm
inasmuch
information
junk
lamb
lumber
making
met
miss
neat
nor
noted
November
object
ours
packed
pearl
pencil
picking
plan
played
poorly
porch
politics
prove
providing
rabbit
reaches
reserve
right
sash
seal
secure
several
sight
someone
sore
speed
suppose
surface
temple
through
tie
township
toy
travel

turn
turned
velvet
voter
watching
weary
weekly
wishes
woven
youth

89%

absent
action
afraid
amounting
answering
anyhow
anyway
anywhere
apart
attend
begin
bottom
bugs
button
cared
central
cheer
chill
clearly
closing
comfort
deliver
detail
devoted
during
factor
feeder
foolish
force
German
glee
helped
hurry
idea
I'll
improved
intended
invite
knew
ladies
language
latter
leaf
lodge
loud
lung

meantime
mistake
nap
notice
orange
painter
pavement
posted
presented
prize
property
raw
reduction
regret
relation
riding
rip
score
seemed
setting
shape
stair
steel
suit
thirty
thus
together
tried
valley
won
won't

88%

acre
acted
against
artist
blew
boiler
careful
climate
colt
dancing
delivered
dodge
election
enclosed
except
fashion
field
fifth
find
forth
greatest
grew
hardware
hotel
household

improve
inclosed
increasing
industry
inform
informed
intend
kindest
later
latest
local
message
movement
moving
noticed
organ
owned
perhaps
phoned
placed
plum
properly
proud
recovered
reduced
repeat
result
retail
returning
ribbon
rye
says
silence
suffering
talked
text
throat
treatment
trouble
uniform
wait
warm
witch
worm

87%

across
attending
begun
bigger
birth
bluff
cause
concluded
cousin
discovered
duties
example

expressed	tiny	modern	enjoying
finest	useful	Mrs.	entering
finger	visiting	narrow	firm
fix	writer	odd	fitting
ford		owe	illness
future	STEP 8—84%	pastor	inspector
gas		peace	instruction
gasoline	*86%*	perfect	ironing
geography	adjust	permit	length
graze	admit	piano	linen
health	advice	pleasure	main
helpful	afterward	prevented	mister
highest	apply	promotion	mountain
holiday	await	quickly	parlor
include	awaiting	quoted	perfectly
inviting	barley	rack	placing
kept	beauty	saver	prepared
known	beet	shade	promised
laugh	built	skirt	prospect
lighting	capital	stating	running
liked	carrier	student	saddle
lonesome	checked	throughout	slide
lucky	coach	too	steady
maid	common	topic	though
married	condition	total	tired
middle	credit	turkey	traveling
month	dairy	visited	voice
monthly	deportment	wage	weight
northern	dice	waist	women
nurse	directed	wasn't	wonderful
offered	eager	whom	
opening	eleventh	workmanship	*84%*
powder	else	worse	advanced
pretty	fifteen		afloat
private	figured	*85%*	ans.
proven	film	account	baking
raising	final	adopted	barrel
rapid	flour	advising	beyond
rapidly	following	aware	breaking
record	football	badly	bulk
refuse	general	balance	butcher
relationship	germ	base	chairman
reliable	globe	bit	chose
required	gown	brown	circus
Saturday	guess	carried	clerk
scare	handled	coming	clever
settlement	honor	comply	collect
since	housekeeping	containing	color
single	ideal	conversation	dealer
sock	improving	cough	decline
soldier	investment	covered	district
spread	lecture	debate	dwelling
storm	lie	deserve	forwarding
strike	lonely	directly	frankly
stuff	lowest	dirty	handling
submit	machine	disposed	handsome
suitable	manage	drilling	healthy
		eighteen	herein

husband
inclose
included
instruct
letting
million
model
needing
nevertheless
ordered
penny
performed
personal
primary
protected
publisher
regulation
renewed
simply
sis
slept
spare
stamped
statement
supply
sure
taxes
thereof
upper
view
winner
worry

83%

abstract
ache
advantage
although
ample
animal
appeal
arrange
automobile
backed
beaten
breakfast
cheerful
companion
delayed
elected
feel
fourteen
fourth
fund
furnishing
habit
important

inclosing
knot
neighbor
notion
outlined
owner
parties
pertaining
proof
pupil
quiet
quite
recess
refreshment
refund
resulting
roll
served
shoulder
sign
skating
success
that's
unpaid
until
written

82%

adventure
boarding
buyer
candle
cement
couple
debating
depot
education
explained
famous
forward
foundation
gotten
haven't
headquarter
homestead
insert
limb
limit
method
minute
moral
needed
neglect
past
plainly
presume
promise

question
scarce
server
serving
sew
sitting
sorrow
standard
stories
throw
tread
weighed
worthy
yoke
you'll

STEP 9—79%

81%

agreeable
agreed
avenue
blessed
bowl
break
captain
caught
collection
connect
considering
coy
curtain
delivery
dose
effort
excess
expected
expecting
explain
factories
fault
feature
furnace
future
guide
headache
hurried
instructed
I've
mass
misses
needle
o'clock
oversight
pattern
post office
problem

prompt
quantity
reputation
ruin
secured
select
sewing
struck
supplied
term
we'll
writing ✓

80%

addition
aid
Ave.
average
booth
chief
convention
crazy
desired
direction
division
either
enclosing
excited
fare
female
fern
forwarded
greatly
grip
group
growth
hospital
inquire
loss
minister
ought
picnic
prepare
profit
resident
settled
shown
sleet
utmost
vision
woman
yourselves

79%

adjustment
ankle
attention
bog

burden
buying
cellar
colored
constant
correction
crew
different
dreadful
earnest
entertainment
favorable
favored
fee
fitted
forenoon
fortune
friendship
furnished
happened
human
intention
invoice
manner
mention
natural
oblige
obtained
opened
reception
recite
refused
remember
rendered
rough
scrap
seldom
tanning
telephone
Thanksgiving
toward
trial
volume
Wednesday

78%

according
actor
adjusted
blackberries
blooming
cherries
cigar
comfortable
complete
confined
crippled

crowd
destroyed
due
forty
further
gland
humor
instant
manufacture
mentioned
musical
namely
neighborhood
parent
patient
preacher
promptly
quit
rainy
recently
regarding
represent
section
shipping
shock
special
waste
Xmas.

77%

addresses
allow
arrive
assure
buggy
carefully
certainly
consist
current
dangerous
director
entered
extended
federal
forced
handkerchief
hare
hers
I'd
installed
isn't
lbs.
loan
loving
machinery
obliged
particular

piece
progress
putting
reasonable
regard
regular
remembering
replying
republican
route
selection
service
situation
subscriber
sweater
tight
touch
truly
weigh
worst
wouldn't

STEP 10—73%

76%

applied
attached
attempt
cabinet
certain
choose
consider
construction
convince
creep
domestic
employed
entitle
failure
fairly
fullest
garage
gee
grocery
interesting
level
likely
measure
owing
popular
prayer
prepaid
priced
produce
receive
slippery
smooth

towel
voting
watched

75%

accept
accomplish
addressed
appointment
assist
attractive
biggest
closely
connecting
connection
constantly
couldn't
creamery
doubt
effect
enroll
entertaining
entire
exactly
figuring
gentleman
hasn't
honestly
hoping
interested
international
its
moderate
ourselves
per cent
position
produced
publication
represented
rifle
studied
supplies
surprise
tickled
transfer
wondering

74%

absolute
automatic
avoid
collar
commerce
complaint
courage
deserved
drama
entry
fever

filing
importance
independent
internal
jury
laid
largely
loose
madam
manager
neglected
opera
parcel
procured
quarter
quote
refer
register
seller
shopping
strength
supervision
to-morrow
tract
Tues.
usual
violin
we've
whose
you'd

73%
appointed
Bro.
calm
circulation
correctly
dependent
difference
easily
extensive
ghost
gravy
hadn't
increase
justified
nineteen
organized
president
proceed
queer
signed
sire
slightly
spirit
treasurer
using

72%
advertise
arranged
arrived
attraction
bargain
choice
circular
college
commence
composition
concern
conclusion
considered
cute
desiring
durable
encourage
enrolled
entertain
entirely
exception
exciting
expired
followed
freight
gentlemen
hesitate
improvement
liberal
neither
preparing
Prof.
remained
rural
selected
shipper
slight
social
stayed
style
surprised
telegram
therefore

71%
ability
absence
accident
actual
advise
advised
aren't
argument
booster
braid
channel
confident

consideration
debt
decided
deposit
described
exam.
favorite
hello
increased
indicate
interest
introduced
issue
pardon
period
remembered
remit
satisfied
splendid
strict
struggle
supposed
taste
wearing

70%
appeared
assured
awful
carrying
considerable
contrary
control
course
credited
crowded
employer
explaining
explanation
expression
forgotten
funeral
instance
introduction
Latin
limited
maybe
medicine
nervous
notify
occupied
passed
positive
prevail
reservation
satisfaction
separate
straight

support
vacant

STEP 11—*66%*

69%
accordingly
approved
attain
bracelet
calves
cedar
collecting
combination
connected
convinced
copies
corrected
doubtless
earliest
enrollment
February
furniture
graduating
grammar
gratitude
guest
lately
library
lovingly
realize
relieve
satisfactory
search
securing
serious
system
themselves
weren't
whether

68%
capable
citizen
concerning
daddy
discontinued
elsewhere
graduation
invitation
item
liquid
numerous
obligation
possible
published
really

shipped
superior
67%
advancement
advertised
attended
believe
continued
didn't
exact
examination
examined
frequently
generous
hustling
impossible
influence
manufacturing
ninth
operated
profitable
recent
reference
satisfy
66%
applicant
available
celebrate
companies
confirm
contemplated
Dr.
federation
maintain
national
opinion
policy
quotation
remedy
requirement
resigned
society
vary
wholesale
65%
agriculture
alley
canned
concert
fashionable
formerly
heir
insurance
involved
niece
patent
pleasant

received
salesman
theater
transportation
valuable
64%
additional
arrival
article
assembly
clothe
decide
decrease
deliveries
evidence
genuine
happiness
hereby
honorable
inclined
investigate
management
misunderstanding
patron
purchased
purpose
raiser
realizing
signature
studying
worried
63%
affair
arriving
attach
banquet
brief
confer
design
destination
disgusted
exercise
graduate
inquiry
junior
purchase
registered
respectfully
source
strawberries
submitted

STEP 12—58%
62%
altogether
billed

cashier
choosing
conference
customer
discourage
envelope
fabric
knowledge
lose
missed
possibly
prefer
profession
regardless
salary
sincere
suggested
transit
61%
advertising
alfalfa
allowed
announce
believing
congratulate
corporation
examiner
expensive
fierce
liable
mamma
mental
operation
process
receiving
reliability
60%
activity
application
cartoon
develop
engineer
establish
expense
glorious
haste
legal
nephew
operating
safety
sanitary
stomach
tatting
terrible
59%
Christian
democrat

doesn't
evidently
identify
jobber
material
various
58%
anxious
assistant
candidate
compelled
cushion
difficult
equipment
excellent
exceptional
investigation
majority
practice
proposition
relative
strictly
successful
welfare
57%
assortment
democratic
electrical
entitled
equally
impression
inducement
instructor
instrument
lining
literary
manual
mere
meter
presence
previous
qualities
representation
senior
series
timothy
worrying
56%
character
confidence
development
etc.
examine
foreign
government
hauled

imagine
organize
personality
renewal
stopped
succeed

55%
acceptance
ambition
amendment
bass
business
catalogue
choir
confirming
constitution
difficulty
disease
error
extreme
generally
issued
losing
magazine
orchestra
politics
prosperous
regularly
te ritory
type
variety

STEP 13—50%

54%
assigned
authorized
beginning
benefit
crochet
customary
favorably
merchandise
ninety
occasion
original
possession
similar
succeeded

53%
awfully
completely
considerably
decision
demonstrated
description
disposal

established
exclusively
gradually
notified
particularly
planning
principal
readily
suggest
supervisor
university

52%
advertisement
assistance
blizzard
calendar
commercial
data
estimated
responsible
sense
stationary
talent
universal

51%
appearance
crocheting
ere
fortunate
inferior
label
meant
nickel
practicing
probably

50%
admission
agency
appreciate
assurance
barely
carnival
coarse
excitement
registration
sympathy

49%
announcement
attendance
attitude
contemplating
duplicate
engineering
heretofore
institution
urge

48%
accomplished
acknowledge
attorney
consultation
co-operation
disappoint
distribution
electricity
existing
experience
illustrated
preliminary
premium
relieved
Sabbath
straightened
usually

47%
congratulation
consequently
enormous
installment
librarian
naturally
ordinary
secretary
superintendent

46%
assignment
assuring
based
council
disagreeable
employee
exhibit
girlie
good-bye
grateful
hastily
illustrating
preparation
resource
semester

STEP 14—42%

45%
administration
appreciation
athletics
cordial
planned
practical

44%
appreciated
civics

co-operative
coupon
finally
literature
merit

43%
administrator
approval
auditor
certificate
co-operating
correspond
familiar
journal
legislation
merely
organization
quantity
response
surgery
surplus

42%
accordance
arrangement
circumstances
conservatory
correspondent
individual
justify
principle

41%
agricultural
assume
auntie
demonstration
extension
illustration
immense
inquires
necessary
remembrance
subscription
substitute
unusual

40%
commission
communication
mechanical
practically
prior
receipt
remittance

39%
actually
continuous
epidemic

The Iowa Spelling Scales

possess
professional
science
specification
vicinity

38%
advisable
all right
authority
ballot
basis
geometry
interfere
rec'd
scientific

STEP 15—34%

37%
absolutely
annually
associated
exhausted
official
regretting

36%
acquainted
consequence
inst.
judgment
permanent
specially
thesis

35%
ambitious
annual
bureau
client
convenient
cordially
disappointed
immediate
institute
personally
physician
possibility
quantities
representative

thorough
X-ray

34%
compliment
exceptionally
executed
executive
license
notary
sufficient

33%
allotment
associate
materially
occasionally
opportunity

32%
acquaintance
algebra
courteous
financial
sincerely

31%
accredited
acquire
alumni
association
disappointment
enthusiastic
extremely
leisure
prosperity

STEP 16—27%

30%
circuit
soliciting

29%
affectionately
anticipating
capacity
commissioner
unusually

28%
bonus
community

immediately
recommend
referred
responsibility
satisfactorily

27%
bulletin
canvass
conveniently
fraternally
referring

26%
candidacy
committee
equipped
inconvenience
maturity
necessity
physical
tuberculosis

25%
campaign
correspondence
especially
fundamental
privilege
solicit

24%
anticipate
assessment
confirmation
enthusiasm
grippe

STEP 17—21%

23%
accompanying
convenience
essential
exhibition
Hallowe'en
originally

22%
definite
mortgage
politician

21%
accommodate
appreciating

20%
affidavit
analysis
chautauqua
unnecessary

19%
recommendation

STEP 18—16%

18%
apparatus
pneumonia

17%
anniversary
appendicitis
guarantee
lieutenant
thoroughly

16%
efficient
zephyr

STEP 19—12%

13%
definitely
phosphorus

11%
characteristic

10%
ingredients
rheumatism

STEP 20—8%

9%
efficiency
guaranteed
peculiarities
schedule

SECTION XIV

THE IOWA SPELLING SCALE

GRADE VII

GRADE VII

Step 1—100%

able
about
adding
afternoon
again
age
air
all
alone
an
are
arm
art
asking
at
be
because
bell
best
better
bill
black
book
box
boy
brain
bring
but
call
called
came
can
car
card
case
charge
class
coat
come
corn
could
country
cut
day
deep
did
do
dog
early
eat
every
eye
fail

fall
farm
fast
faster
fell
fellow
fish
five
forgive
from
gate
get
girl
give
glove
go
gold
good
got
grade
grain
had
half
hand
happy
have
help
helping
her
him
his
home
hot
how
ice
if
inside
into
is
it
June
just
kind
land
large
last
late
left
lesson
let
letter
like
little
live

long
looking
lot
make
man
many
master
me
milk
more
most
mother
must
my
name
neck
net
Nov.
nut
old
on
one
out
paper
park
pay
people
pick
pig
place
pleased
point
postage
put
reading
rest
row
rule
run
school
see
sell
send
she
silk
sister
six
snow
some
space
stage
start
started
state

stick
stone
such
take
taken
teaching
tell
test
that
the
then
think
thinking
this
time
top
toy
train
tree
unable
unless
up
us
very
wall
was
way
we
well
west
what
when
while
who
why
wife
will
window
winter
with
without
word
work
working
year
yellow
your

Step 2—99%

above
active
add
added

The Iowa Spelling Scales

after	display	light	railroad
ago	doing	longer	rain
ahead	down	longest	rate
along	dress	look	reach
also	drop	love	read
am	each	loved	real
answer	earth	mad	red
any	east	made	report
ask	edge	mail	ride
away	eight	mailed	ring
baby	eighty	maker	river
back	face	market	rock
backing	farming	may	rush
bad	fat	meal	rust
band	fight	mean	sad
bank	filled	mill	said
banker	finding	Monday	Sat.
bean	fine	money	sat
bed	flat	mostly	saw
been	food	much	say
behind	for	mud	saying
belonging	found	music	seat
below	free	myself	self
big	game	night	shall
bird	getting	nine	sheep
birthday	given	north	ship
blank	glad	not	shoe
blue	going	note	short
bought	gone	notice	should
bright	grant	number	showed
bringing	green	oats	sick
brother	handed	of	sign
bunch	hang	oil	sixty
butter	has	older	slow
by	he	oldest	snowed
calf	head	our	so
cannot	hill	outside	son
cap	holding	oven	song
cash	hour	over	sound
catch	house	overcoat	spell
cent	however	pack	spend
child	ill	page	sport
children	in	paying	spot
clean	ink	payment	spring
clear	Jan.	pen	stamp
close	joy	picking	stand
cold	July	pie	standing
cost	kindly	plate	stay
cream	kiss	play	still
cross	lace	playing	store
cup	lady	please	subject
dandy	lake	poor	summer
danger	landing	press	Sunday
dear	larger	print	sweet
December	law	proper	swell
dinner	leader	quick	table
discount	leave	rail	thank

thanking	April	delighted	income
them	as	died	inspect
they	Aug.	dispose	invited
thing	aunt	door	January
three	bake	drill	jump
till	ball	drug	keep
tire	bat	drum	keeping
told	battle	dust	kid
took	become	easy	kill
town	bee	end	kinder
trip	behalf	evening	kindness
trust	belt	ever	king
trusting	beside	example	labor
try	blood	exchange	ladies
twice	boat	express	lay
two	body	far	learned
under	booklet	fear	leather
use	boss	feed	life
vacation	bother	feet	lived
value	bottle	felt	liver
walk	boxes	fill	lives
want	branch	filling	living
washing	brush	finish	loaded
week	building	first	lost
went	burn	fishing	luck
were	cake	Friday	mark
whatever	calling	friend	marking
wheat	camp	fully	May
whenever	care	gift	meat
where	carpet	glass	meet
white	chair	glasses	mine
wide	chance	goat	Miss
willing	change	goose	mouth
win	check	grand	Mr.
wind	city	grandfather	nation
wise	classes	granted	near
wish	closed	great	nearly
wishing	cloth	hair	never
wood	club	harder	new
world	coal	hardly	news
would	coffee	hat	nobody
wrote	coin	hay	noon
yard	conduct	hearing	off
yes	contest	heat	once
yet	continue	heating	only
you	cook	heavy	or
zone	counting	here	other
	covering	herself	packing
STEP 3—98%	cow	high	paint
	cutting	hit	painted
act	dance	hog	part
agent	dark	holder	party
almost	darling	hundred	pass
amount	date	hunt	peach
and	deal	hunting	pine
another	Dec.	inch	placed
apple	delay	inches	planted

The Iowa Spelling Scales

pole	spelling	army	father
post	stood	auto	Feb.
pretty	stop	awhile	feel
printed	storm	banking	few
printing	stunt	barn	fifty
provide	sugar	basket	finished
race	sum	bay	fit
raised	sunshine	bear	flower
range	talk	before	folder
rank	talking	begin	foot
ready	tank	being	forget
reduction	telling	belong	four
remain	ten	bench	frost
remove	tested	bet	gain
removal	thin	between	garden
rent	thousand	block	garment
renting	ticket	born	gather
request	to-day	brick	gave
respect	ton	bushel	glee
rich	travel	button	grass
rolling	treat	buy	ground
room	true	cared	growing
round	trunk	cattle	hall
safe	Tuesday	caused	handy
same	twenty	chain	hard
sample	united	chum	hate
sand	used	church	hear
saved	valued	clay	held
seed	visit	clearly	higher
seeing	voter	clock	himself
sending	walked	cloudy	hold
sent	walking	coast	homesick
set	wanting	colder	horse
seven	war	company	I'm
seventh	wash	contain	iron
seventy	washed	cotton	island
shade	watch	count	job
shipment	western	cover	judge
show	which	crop	kitten
shut	wild	dad	know
silver	wool	daughter	largest
sin	worked	dearest	learn
singing	write	deed	leg
single	yearly	demand	less
sink	yesterday	depend	lift
sit	yourself	direct	list
size		dodge	listed
slip	Step 4—96%	dollar	load
small		don't	local
snowing	97%	dozen	locate
soap		dream	location
soft	abstract	drilling	looked
sold	advance	drive	low
soon	aim	egg	lower
sooner	alive	election	lunch
sort	always	family	machine
south	anyone	farmer	maid
	anywhere		

mailing
March
matter
membership
morning
move
moved
nature
nice
no
noted
nothing
November
now
object
Oct.
office
orange
order
outfit
painting
pair
papa
per
picture
pin
pink
plan
pleasure
plenty
poorly
pound
prevent
price
protest
reached
reaches
reader
recall
recover
remark
renew
reported
require
required
respond
result
retain
return
rice
road
rose
rye
sack
secure
seem
selling

September
serve
settle
several
share
sheet
sickness
side
sleep
smart
soil
someone
something
sometime
spending
spent
standard
stated
station
staying
steam
step
stove
stranger
strongest
stuff
suffering
sun
teacher
teeth
tenth
than
thereafter
thick
those
thought
thread
thus
to-night
total
township
trace
twelve
uncle
understanding
understood
union
velvet
vote
wagon
waiting
wanted
watching
water
welcome
wet
wheel

wire
within
worker

96%

anybody
anything
around
asleep
backed
became
branches
brand
brought
busy
carry
center
changed
charged
cheer
chicken
Christmas
cleaner
cleaning
cooking
cord
cottage
crib
cure
damp
dare
dealing
deeply
degree
desire
die
directed
doctor
done
dressed
ease
English
enter
even
extra
fact
farther
fence
figure
find
fire
follow
forgot
former
fort
fruit
fun

funny
gladly
greater
grove
grown
handle
happen
hardware
heard
hen
hence
highest
history
honest
hurt
improve
improved
industry
instead
jar
joined
learning
liberty
lumber
making
match
mate
meeting
message
mighty
million
mind
named
nerve
next
nicely
none
nor
normal
nose
obtain
October
open
ordering
overlooked
packed
partly
patch
payable
pencil
person
phone
potatoes
present
primary
produce
product

The Iowa Spelling Scales

profit	trying	depending	needed
provided	understand	deportment	noise
Pump	upon	does	ocean
pure	voice	draft	offering
quart	waited	dread	oh
queen	whereby	earning	otherwise
question	wished	enjoying	own
raise	wishes	enough	package
record	won	except	pain
reduce	worth	excuse	passing
regulation	young	extend	pillow
relationship	zero	extent	pocket
render		factory	postal
rented	Step 5—94%	failed	post card
renter		famous	power
requested	95%	favor	presume
returned	acting	feeling	prize
roof	action	file	program
rubber	address	fix	progress
rug	afraid	floor	public
scale	agree	form	pull
scare	anyhow	formed	raw
second	apart	frame	reaching
seemed	arrived	fresh	reason
seen	August	friendly	regret
Sept.	badly	fur	reply
shame	base	furnish	rushed
shape	beat	gown	score
shot	beg	grandma	scout
sight	begun	grew	season
simple	bid	guess	shop
sir	birth	hoped	skate
smaller	blame	hotel	sorry
snap	blow	insist	speaker
somewhat	bottom	joke	square
somewhere	bridge	killed	suit
speak	broke	kitchen	team
special	brown	knowing	tent
spoke	build	known	thankful
spread	can't	language	thirty
stair	cause	laugh	through
starting	central	length	Thursday
steady	chapter	letting	tie
stock	charming	likewise	trade
street	chop	located	treatment
study	cities	lone	turned
supper	clothing	lonesome	wake
sure	colt	loud	warm
taking	content	lovely	weary
talked	contract	lowest	weather
temple	cooler	lump	wedding
there	court	maple	whole
these	damage	mind	witch
third	dated	might	withdraw
tile	debate	month	worm
tip	debating	monthly	woven
treated	decline		wrong

The Iowa Spelling Scales

94%

among
answered
attend
beef
began
Bible
bite
board
boiler
broken
builder
bulk
cat
chart
climate
comfort
cool
county
dead
dearly
deliver
devoted
duty
eighteen
elect
elected
else
everything
expert
explain
feature
fifteen
fifth
figured
fixed
flavor
flour
forest
froze
frozen
gallon
general
gray
greatest
ha
harvest
heap
hole
I'd
illness
including
increase
instruct
itself
join
joyful

knew
lame
leaving
lighting
listen
lodge
loving
lucky
ma
married
meantime
member
mistake
mister
northern
notify
notion
opened
ordered
pearl
pending
played
powder
presented
prevented
production
ranch
recovered
refused
relation
remind
repair
repeat
rip
shortly
sixth
sock
studies
supply
taxes
tried
trouble
turn
uniform
valley
visited
visiting
watched
weak
worry
youth

STEP 6—92%

93%

account
actor
addition

advantage
already
ample
animal
ans.
answering
aside
asked
ate
bugs
cane
cheap
checked
collect
copy
correct
cough
daily
dealer
district
division
domestic
dreadful
dresser
during
duties
education
eleventh
expressed
factor
fancy
female
field
film
folk
football
force
front
geography
having
herewith
homestead
human
hurry
idea
include
indeed
informed
invite
justify
kisses
leaves
lecture
loyal
measure
model
moderate

moment
movement
narrow
natural
nearer
neat
newspaper
odd
officer
pavement
plum
printer
promotion
quickly
quoted
rack
raining
recess
refuse
requesting
retail
returning
rod
rough
running
sale
served
serving
settlement
sewing
shock
sorrow
stamped
stories
strongly
student
tend
term
their
throughout
tiny
to
track
training
turkey
unpaid
useful
winner
wonder
wonderful
worthy

92%

absent
acre
afterward
aid
arrive

The Iowa Spelling Scales

artist	kept	attending	refreshment
attraction	kindest	beaten	regular
barley	lamb	beyond	reliable
barrel	latest	boarding	reserve
beet	least	breakfast	says
bit	liberal	built	shipping
blessed	lonely	candle	silence
blew	lung	caught	simply
bluff	manage	circulation	since
both	merry	circus	skirt
broad	middle	color	speed
burden	modern	common	taste
carried	moving	concluded	taught
cast	need	condition	tax
changing	needle	containing	trained
cheaper	offered	conversation	until
checking	organ	creamery	upper
cigar	ours	dairy	wage
cleaned	painter	detail	written
clerk	parties	difference	
closer	peace	discovered	Step 7—88%
coach	perfect	encourage	*90%*
coasting	permit	enjoyed	
companion	pools	entering	according
complete	private	expected	anyway
connecting	prompt	expression	appeal
corner	properly	feeder	ashamed
corrected	prospect	final	attention
covered	proved	followed	aware
credit	rained	foolish	booth
dancing	remember	forth	butcher
death	riding	greeting	buying
delivered	right	habit	chill
directly	sash	household	connect
enjoy	saving	ideal	connected
eve	seal	inform	connection
everybody	setting	intended	couple
everyone	shed	ivory	crazy
feeding	shoulder	junk	delayed
finest	steel	leaf	delightful
finger	suitable	main	dirty
flesh	surface	miss	eager
foundation	though	nevertheless	effort
frankly	throat	owe	enclosed
freeze	title	pastor	entertainment
French	topic	posted	expecting
furnace	wait	pride	fairly
gained	wear	problem	fortune
goldfish	worse	promise	friendship
greatly	writer	protected	fuel
headache		proud	fund
health	*91%*	prove	furnished
honor	advising	proven	gaining
husband	against	pupil	gas
important	although	quotation	gentleman
information	amounting	rabbit	German
inviting	appear	reduced	gotten
	apply		

grind
grit
grocery
healthy
I'll
included
investment
later
level
liked
liquid
met
minute
neglect
neglected
noticed
obtained
owner
penny
period
phoned
piano
porch
prepaid
providing
putting
raising
rapid
rapidly
refund
remained
resulting
saddle
section
secured
sis
slept
slipper
smooth
social
statement
suppose
Thanksgiving
vision
weigh
weight
whom
women
wondering

89%
absolute
across
addresses
adjust
advised
arrange
assure

author
automobile
beauty
careful
closely
contained
current
curtain
dangerous
debt
direction
entered
failure
fair
fashion
fee
fierce
forgotten
further
germ
globe
grammar
graze
guide
handling
helped
hereafter
hesitate
honestly
inclosed
instruction
isn't
jury
loss
method
mountain
Mrs.
nap
neighbor
opening
owned
pa
per cent
picnic
plain
popular
property
recite
regard
ribbon
settled
sore
strike
struggle
style
sweater
text

thereof
too
tread
trial
wasn't
won't
worst

88%
acted
admit
advanced
adventure
allow
attended
Ave.
avenue
bigger
break
buggy
cement
certain
chairman
cherries
chief
comply
composition
consider
considered
correctly
cousin
crew
didn't
difficult
dwelling
entire
exact
explained
fault
following
forty
forwarding
fullest
furnishing
future
gasoline
gland
happened
hare
helpful
herein
holiday
housekeeping
increasing
inspector
instructed
lie
limb

mass
national
nurse
outlined
parlor
perhaps
plow
possible
prepare
president
promised
rainy
register
renewed
reputation
scrap
seldom
server
service
skating
slightly
soldier
success
therefore
tired
treasurer

87%
agreeable
agreed
ambition
appointed
approved
assist
average
await
awaiting
baking
balance
blackberries
blooming
buyer
cabinet
calm
carefully
cheerful
collection
coming
commerce
consideration
considering
construction
convention
correction
depot
desired
dice
director

The Iowa Spelling Scales

due	clever	copies	colored
enclosing	closing	drama	comfortable
entirely	commence	excess	confined
entitle	courage	favorable	constantly
excited	described	federal	continued
expired	deserve	forced	cute
firm	different	forward	decided
fitted	dose	forwarded	discourage
fitting	earliest	fourteen	either
funeral	effect	growth	enrolled
gentlemen	fare	inclose	error
ghost	fourth	increased	extended
impossible	garage	indicate	favored
improving	gee	intend	federation
inquire	graduation	international	group
ironing	grip	knot	hospital
limit	guest	lately	importance
machinery	handled	limited	inasmuch
manufacture	handsome	linen	inclosing
needing	headquarter	minister	insert
numerous	humor	musical	I've
parent	hurried	namely	misunderstanding
pertaining	intention	obliged	past
placing	interest	o'clock	patent
position	issue	ought	piece
prayer	latter	ourselves	process
prepared	manner	produced	purpose
preparing	oversight	publication	queer
priced	parcel	quality	received
promptly	performed	represented	reception
proof	personal	rifle	relative
publisher	plainly	roll	representation
quiet	post office	route	republican
quite	proceed	select	resident
reasonable	published	seller	saver
Saturday	recently	signed	scarce
sew	represent	sleet	society
slide	selected	strawberries	system
spare	selection	suggest	tanning
strength	situation	themselves	telegram
struck	traveling	together	telephone
submit	whose	to-morrow	that's
throw	yourselves	towel	tract
touch	*85%*	volume	waste
transportation	ache	woman	Wednesday
truly	advertised	wouldn't	workmanship
view	appeared	*84%*	*83%*
waist	avoid	adjusted	absence
weekly	believe	advertise	capable
weighed	bowl	advice	circular
yoke	breaking	advise	citizen
	capital	afloat	confident
Step 8—84%	celebrate	ankle	creep
	chose	applied	crippled
86%	complaint	approval	doubtless
banquet	consist	carrier	earnest
bog	constant	cashier	enclose

enroll
exam.
exciting
factories
graduate
graduating
gratitude
instance
insurance
interesting
knowledge
laid
legal
manager
manufacturing
misses
owing
particular
preacher
receive
ruin
satisfied
search
shipper
shopping
shone
stating
supplied
supposed
tight
violin

82%
accept
accomplish
addressed
adopted
appointment
arranged
arriving
assured
assuring
attached
attempt
awful
biggest
cellar
collecting
concern
design
easily
employed
entertain
ford
generous
hoping
improvement
instant

internal
material
mention
neither
oblige
perfectly
purchase
quarter
recent
remembered
remit
replying
resigned
salary
securing
subscriber
surprise
worried
writing

STEP 9—79%

81%
assembly
bracelet
cartoon
companies
conference
delivery
develop
disposed
doubt
entertaining
fern
fever
freight
handkerchief
happiness
invitation
item
loan
loose
mentioned
nephew
operated
passed
pattern
prevail
realize
regardless
satisfactory
serious
sitting
slight
spirit
supplies
support

theater
tickled
toward
usual
vacant
we'll
Xmas.

80%
actual
adjustment
appreciate
article
attractive
booster
canned
captain
course
credited
desiring
exercise
extensive
fabric
figuring
forenoon
hello
inclined
interested
jobber
justified
library
likely
manual
notified
positive
quit
raiser
remembering
rendered
source
superior
universal
wearing
you'll

79%
agriculture
attach
attain
authorized
automatic
calves
choose
collar
concerning
convince
coy
decrease
dependent

deposit
destroyed
explaining
filing
hadn't
haven't
hereby
independent
institution
introduction
lovingly
management
moral
neighborhood
occupied
opinion
patient
regarding
requirement
rural
stayed
studied
voting

78%
ability
agency
argument
certainly
college
conclusion
considerable
convinced
couldn't
daddy
difficulty
entry
established
exception
favorite
finally
hasn't
heir
involved
lbs.
nineteen
opera
ordinary
procured
sanitary
stationary
straight
tatting
Tues.
utmost
we've
whether

The Iowa Spelling Scales

77%
accident
activity
affair
arrival
channel
concert
contemplated
crowd
deliveries
democratic
deserved
destination
durable
establish
evidence
exactly
examined
February
hustling
junior
liable
lining
maybe
nervous
policy
Prof.
purchased
quote
slippery
supervision
using
you'd

STEP 10—73%

76%
application
brief
Bro.
choice
compelled
customer
decide
formerly
hauled
investigate
investigation
literary
madam
maintain
mamma
mere
obligation
operating
operation
pleasant

proposition
refer
regularly
satisfaction
transfer
university

75%
allowed
anxious
assistant
blizzard
character
Christian
confer
confidence
crowded
discontinued
duplicate
expense
explanation
favorably
haste
influence
installed
introduced
journal
largely
organized
registered
relieve
series
signature
sire
strict
surprised
transit

74%
advertising
cedar
combination
development
Dr.
employer
engineer
envelope
expensive
frequently
gravy
honorable
illustrating
its
merchandise
pardon
possibly
remedy
shipped
submitted

suggested
territory
valuable
vary
wholesale
worrying

73%
choosing
commercial
coupon
cushion
description
enrollment
fashionable
government
hers
impression
instrument
issued
Latin
meant
ninth
orchestra
previous
profitable
Prosperous
realizing
receiving
responsible
type
vicinity

72%
accordance
admission
alfalfa
announce
applicant
bargain
based
believing
disagreeable
disposal
elsewhere
examination
examine
extreme
fortunate
glorious
illustration
imagine
majority.
medicine
mental
profession
qualities
really
reference

respectfully
salesman

71%
assurance
barely
billed
braid
business
confirming
control
democrat
genuine
identify
personality
principal
reliability
reservation
satisfy
senior
strictly
usually
weren't

70%
advancement
alley
altogether
carrying
contemplating
contrary
disgusted
electrical
entitled
evidently
furniture
institute
literature
practice
premium
sincere
splendid

STEP 11—66%

69%
accordingly
benefit
candidate
choir
circumstances
considerably
doesn't
equally
equipment
gradually
invoice
missed
politics

presence
similar
stomach
terrible
various
68%
accomplished
available
estimated
label
niece
separate
successful
67%
advisable
appreciated
constitution
engineering
etc.
exceptional
instructor
patron
prosperity
substitute
welfare
66%
assignment
clothe
demonstrated
distribution
employee
magazine
mechanical
practical
preparation
subscription
succeed
sympathy
variety
65%
amendment
congratulation
data
exclusively
experience
illustrated
lose
prefer
resource
studying
succeeded
surplus
unusual
64%
associated
assortment

attitude
bass
capacity
coarse
corporation
electricity
executed
foreign
generally
inquiry
practicing
registration
renewal
stopped
63%
administration
assistance
auditor
awfully
basis
civics
confirm
congratulate
examiner
librarian
readily
timothy

Step 12—58%
62%
acknowledge
appearance
aren't
interfere
naturally
nickel
particularly
possession
semester
urge
61%
actually
additional
calendar
certificate
commission
co-operative
customary
exhausted
heretofore
inquiries
losing
ninety
organize
original

60%
absolutely
allotment
assigned
assume
attorney
beginning
conservatory
council
decision
demonstration
excellent
exhibit
inferior
organization
planned
response
safely
supervisor
59%
acquire
appreciation
co-operation
crochet
excitement
existing
inducement
planning
science
secretary
talent
58%
announcement
consequently
consultation
good-bye
individual
maturity
relieved
sense
57%
ballot
carnival
cordial
disappoint
grateful
legislation
remittance
specification
56%
administrator
appreciating
association
co-operating
crocheting
disease

meter
opportunity
probably
55%
acceptance
annual
catalogue
installment
official
practically

Step 13—50%
54%
athletics
completely
hastily
necessity
occasion
personally
preliminary
quantities
quantity
Sabbath
straightened
53%
advertisement
agricultural
bulletin
community
extension
geometry
merit
principle
52%
acquainted
alumni
ambitious
associate
client
compliment
cordially
correspond
referred
remembrance
superintendent
51%
arrangement
campaign
disappointment
enthusiastic
financial
girlie
permanent
50%
bureau
communication

regretting
sincerely
solicit
thorough

49%
enormous
license
materially
necessary
physical
responsibility

48%
all right
ere
exceptionally
familiar
inconvenience
merely
possibility
professional
receipt

47%
auntie
authority
definite
soliciting

46%
attendance
consequence
disappointed
immediately

STEP 14—42%

45%
immediate
rec'd
specially
sufficient
surgery

44%
assessment
extremely
leisure
possess
thoroughly

43%
accredited
annually
anticipate
circuit
epidemic
especially
judgment
notary
satisfactorily

42%
commissioner
correspondent
politician

41%
algebra
bonus
continuous
enthusiasm
prior
privilege

40%
acquaintance
exhibition
immense

39%
canvass
convenient
courteous
recommend
representative
scientific
thesis

38%
executive
originally

STEP 15—34%

37%
analysis
equipped
fundamental
mortgage

36%
fraternally
unusually

35%
efficient
physician

34%
affectionately

33%
committee
correspondence
occasionally
referring
tuberculosis

32%
accommodate
anticipating
apparatus
characteristic
unnecessary

31%
candidacy
confirmation
inst.

STEP 16—27%

30%
efficiency
lieutenant

29%
accompanying
guarantee

28%
convenience
peculiarities —

27%
chautauqua
essential
guaranteed
X-ray

25%
recommendation
schedule

24%
appendicitis
conveniently
pneumonia

STEP 17—21%

23%
anniversary
grippe
rheumatism

21%
Hallowe'en

20%
definitely
ingredients

19%
phosphorus

STEP 18—16%

18%
affidavit

16%
zephyr

SECTION XV

THE IOWA SPELLING SCALE

GRADE VIII

GRADE VIII

Step 1—100%

able	body	dinner	herself
about	book	done	high
above	bottle	dream	hill
add	bought	dust	him
added	box	each	himself
adding	brick	earth	his
advance	bring	east	hog
afternoon	brother	easy	holding
again	bunch	eat	horse
age	but	edge	hot
ago	butter	eighty	house
all	by	end	hunt
alone	call	enjoy	hunting
along	called	eye	ill
am	calling	face	important
an	came	fail	in
and	camp	fall	inches
another	can	farm	ink
anything	car	farming	inside
apple	card	feet	into
are	care	few	is
army	cash	filled	it
around	cause	fine	job
art	cent	fire	July
as	child	fishing	June
ask	children	food	just
at	city	foot	keeping
away	class	form	kid
baby	clean	found	kind
back	clear	free	kinder
backing	close	from	lake
bad	coach	gained	land
ball	coal	get	large
band	cold	girl	last
bank	come	give	late
banking	contest	given	law
bat	corn	go	lay
bay	cost	going	leader
be	country	gone	left
because	cow	good	leg
been	cross	got	less
behind	cup	grade	let
being	dad	grain	letter
bell	danger	greater	life
belong	dare	had	like
below	darling	half	list
best	date	happy	little
better	day	has	live
big	December	hat	lived
bill	decline	have	liver
bird	deed	hay	lives
blank	degree	he	load
	did	head	long
	died	help	look
board		her	looking

126

love	partly	silk	thousand
low	payment	sit	three
mad	pen	six	time
mail	people	size	train
mailing	person	slow	treat
make	pie	small	tree
making	place	smart	trust
man	plate	snow	trusting
many	play	so	trying
market	pleased	soft	twenty
mate	poor	sold	under
may	power	somewhat	understand
me	prevented	sound	understanding
mean	put	spelling	up
membership	question	spend	use
message	rail	spent	value
milk	raised	spoke	waiting
mill	range	sport	walk
mine	read	stamp	wall
money	reader	start	wanted
more	ready	started	was
most	real	starting	wash
mother	reason	state	watch
move	red	stated	water
must	rent	station	way
my	report	stay	we
named	request	stick	well
nature	rest	still	were
nearly	return	stock	what
net	rich	stone	whatever
next	ride	stood	wheat
nice	rock	store	wheel
night	room	storm	when
nine	round	stranger	where
nobody	rug	study	while
noon	rule	subject	who
not	run	such	wife
note	rush	summer	will
nothing	said	sunshine	willing
object	sample	take	wind
office	Sat.	talk	wire
oil	saw	teach	wise
old	say	teaching	with
oldest	school	tell	without
on	see	telling	wood
once	seeing	ten	work
one	send	tent	worked
open	sending	test	worker
order	set	thank	working
out	setting	thanking	world
over	sheep	that	would
overcoat	ship	the	woven
own	shoe	them	wrote
pack	short	thing	year
page	should	think	yellow
painted	show	thinking	yes
paper	sick	this	yet

128 The Iowa Spelling Scales

you
yourself
zone

STEP 2—99%

abstract
account
act
action
address
after
agent
ahead
air
also
amount
answer
any
anybody
anyhow
April
arm
asking
ate
attend
Aug.
aunt
awhile
bake
banker
barn
bottle
bee
before
between
black
block
blood
blue
boat
booklet
boss
bother
boxes
boy
brain
branches
bright
bringing
brush
build
built
bushel
cannot
cap
car

carry
case
catch
cattle
chain
chair
charge
charged
chart
cheer
church
cities
classes
cleaned
clothing
club
coat
coffee
coin
company
conduct
contract
cook
correct
could
count
court
cover
covering
cream
cut
cutting
dandy
dark
dead
deal
dealing
dear
debate
deep
delay
depending
discount
display
district
dog
doing
down
dress
drew
drill
drop
drug
drum
duty
early
earning

evening
ever
every
exchange
expected
express
fact
factory
failed
far
farmer
fast
faster
father
favor
fear
feed
fell
fellow
fight
figure
file
fill
filling
finding
finish
fish
fit
five
flesh
for
force
forgive
formed
fort
Friday
friend
front
gain
gate
gave
gift
glad
glass
glove
goat
gold
goose
green
grew
ground
hair
handed
handy
happen
hard
harder

hate
heard
heat
heavy
helping
here
history
hit
hold
holder
home
hotel
hour
how
however
hundred
hurry
ice
if
inch
instead
instruction
invite
invited
ivory
Jan.
January
joy
judge
keep
kill
kindly
king
kiss
know
lace
ladies
lady
landing
larger
learn
learning
leaving
light
located
longer
longest
looked
lost
lot
loved
lovely
lower
luck
lump
lunch
made

The Iowa Spelling Scales

mailed	playing	settlement	they
maker	please	seven	thin
mark	pleasure	seventy	third
married	pocket	several	those
master	point	shade	thought
match	present	shall	thus
matter	press	shame	ticket
Monday	print	share	tip
mostly	printed	she	to-day
mountain	printer	shut	told
mouth	produce	sickness	took
Mr.	product	silver	top
much	protest	simple	town
mud	provided	sin	township
music	pull	sir	toy
myself	pure	sister	trade
name	quart	sixty	trip
nation	quick	skate	trunk
near	railroad	sleep	try
never	rain	slip	two
new	raise	smaller	unable
nicely	rate	snowing	union
normal	raw	soil	unless
north	reach	some	us
nose	reading	something	used
notice	reduced	sometime	valued
Nov.	reduction	son	wagon
number	remain	song	waited
nut	removed	soon	wake
oats	rented	sooner	walked
Oct.	renting	space	want
of	repeat	spell	wanting
off	reply	spot	war
only	result	spring	warm
outside	rice	square	washing
oven	ring	stage	watching
overlooked	river	stamped	went
packing	rolling	stand	western
paint	roof	standing	white
painting	rubber	staying	why
papa	running	stove	wild
park	rust	strongest	win
part	sack	stunt	window
party	safe	sugar	winter
pass	same	Sunday	wish
patch	sand	sweet	wished
pay	sat	swell	wishes
peace	score	table	wishing
peach	seat	taken	within
personal	second	talking	word
phone	secure	tank	worth
pick	seed	teacher	wrong
picking	self	teeth	yard
picture	sell	tenth	yesterday
pig	selling	than	your
pine	sent	then	zero
placed			

The Iowa Spelling Scales

STEP 3—98%

acre
acted
acting
active
actor
against
aid
alive
among
answered
answering
anyone
anywhere
aside
asleep
auto
aware
backed
basket
bean
bed
began
begun
behalf
belonging
belt
bench
beside
Bible
birthday
blame
born
branch
bridge
broke
broken
brought
building
burn
buy
buying
cake
calf
careful
carpet
cat
caused
center
chance
change
changed
chapter
charming
cheap
check

chicken
chum
cleaner
cleaning
clearly
clerk
closed
cloth
coast
colder
colt
condition
construction
contain
continue
cooking
cool
cord
corrected
cottage
cotton
counting
crop
daily
damage
damp
dance
daughter
dealer
debt
Dec.
delighted
depend
deportment
die
direct
do
don't
door
draft
dresser
drive
egg
eight
eighteen
else
English
entire
even
everything
example
excuse
expecting
extend
family
fat
feeding

feeling
felt
fifty
first
fixed
flat
flower
forget
former
four
frame
French
frost
fruit
fur
furnish
gather
germ
grant
granted
grass
greatest
growing
hand
hang
hardly
hardware
health
heap
hear
heating
held
herewith
highest
hole
honest
idea
improved
income
inform
iron
island
jar
jump
jury
kindness
kitten
lamp
lame
largest
laugh
learned
leather
leave
leaves
lesson
liberty

lift
liked
listed
living
loaded
local
locate
location
loud
lung
machine
maid
maple
March
marking
May
meal
meantime
measure
meat
meet
method
middle
might
mighty
mind
Miss
mistake
month
monthly
morning
moved
neck
news
noise
none
noted
November
now
offering
older
orange
other
our
ours
package
parties
paying
per
pillow
pink
plenty
popular
post
posted
pound
pretty

The Iowa Spelling Scales

prevented	spending	STEP 4—96%	duties
price	steam	97%	ease
printing	step	advanced	education
prize	stop	adventure	elected
production	street	advise	election
promise	strongly	afterward	eleventh
proper	student	agree	enough
property	sum	aim	entered
proud	sun	almost	eve
provide	supper	already	everyone
queen	taxes	ample	excited
race	tested	animal	expert
reached	thereafter	ans.	extent
reaches	thick	appointed	extra
reaching	thirty	base	factor
recall	thread	beat	failure
record	tile	beauty	Feb.
recover	till	beg	female
refuse	tire	begin	fence
regular	ton	bet	film
regulation	topic	blessed	find
relation	trained	blew	finished
remark	travel	blow	folder
remove	treated	bluff	follow
renter	treatment	boiler	forest
repair	true	both	fortune
require	turkey	brand	freeze
reserve	twelve	bugs	fully
respect	twice	builder	fun
respond	understood	button	funny
retail	upon	buyer	furnished
road	valley	calm	gaining
rushed	very	carried	garden
sad	visit	cast	gentleman
sale	vote	cheaper	glasses
saying	voter	checked	glee
season	walking	chill	gotten
section	washed	chop	gown
seen	watched	clay	grand
Sept.	weak	clock	grandfather
September	week	composition	great
seventh	welcome	consider	greatly
shop	west	conversation	hall
shot	wet	crib	handle
showed	whenever	cure	having
side	whereby	dated	hearing
sight	which	dearly	improve
sign	wide	deeply	included
simply	witch	deliver	increase
singing	wonder	depot	inquire
snap	worm	devoted	insist
snowed	worse	direction	inspect
somewhere	write	dodge	instruct
sort	yearly	dose	interest
south	young	dressed	introduced
speed		drilling	issue
		during	itself

I've	requested	beaten	general
joined	required	became	gladly
kitchen	resident	become	gland
knowing	retain	beyond	goldfish
labor	returned	bid	greeting
leaf	right	bigger	harvest
least	rod	birth	helped
lecture	saved	brown	hereafter
letting	scale	buggy	homesick
lone	settle	burden	homestead
lonesome	shed	busy	hoped
lumber	sheet	cared	hurt
meeting	shipment	carrier	ideal
member	shortly	caught	illness
mend	single	cigar	indeed
miss	sink	circus	industry
moment	sixth	closer	information
movement	slipper	collect	inviting
need	sorry	collection	joke
needed	speak	color	kept
needle	special	comfort	killed
nerve	spread	companion	known
obtain	stair	connect	language
October	stories	constant	later
opened	stuff	copy	length
or	suffering	correctly	level
otherwise	suppose	couple	likewise
outfit	tie	cousin	limited
packed	tired	covered	lowest
pain	to	dearest	lucky
passing	total	death	ma
payable	trace	demand	manage
pencil	trouble	desire	mass
per cent	turn	directly	minister
perfect	turned	dispose	minute
pin	united	does	moderate
plain	velvet	dollar	narrow
plan	visiting	dread	nearer
planted	whom	enclose	neat
poorly	withdraw	enjoying	neglected
post card	wonderful	entering	nor
potatoes	wool	everybody	nurse
prefer	youth	expressed	odd
problem		extended	officer
progress	*96%*	federation	ordering
prospect	according	field	ourselves
pump	addition	fifth	owe
putting	addresses	finest	owner
rack	advantage	flavor	pair
rainy	always	floor	particular
ranch	appeal	forgot	pavement
rank	appear	foundation	period
recess	appeared	frankly	phoned
reduce	apply	froze	porch
remind	attended	fund	postage
render	average	gallon	prepare
reputation	barrel	game	president
	bear		

The Iowa Spelling Scales

	STEP 5—94%	farther	owned
pride		feature	painter
primary	95%	feeder	pearl
prompt	absence	feel	pending
properly	accept	fifteen	performed
public	adjust	final	perhaps
rained	advised	fix	piano
raining	afraid	flour	played
rapid	allow	football	possible
refused	amounting	fourteen	postal
relative	anyway	friendly	presented
remained	approved	frozen	produced
remember	arrived	furnishing	program
reported	asked	future	promptly
resulting	August	garage	protected
rip	awaiting	gas	proven
rose	barley	geography	providing
seal	beef	getting	published
seem	beet	globe	pupil
serve	breakfast	graduate	quickly
served	broad	grandma	raising
settled	cane	grit	recovered
shape	cement	guess	regret
shock	central	ha	relationship
signe	checking	habit	rendered
sinced	Christmas	honor	renew
sock	circular	hurried	returning
soldier	climate	husband	ribbon
someone	coasting	I'll	sash
sorrow	commerce	include	saving
speaker	common	including	says
steel	complete	intended	scout
strike	concluded	interested	search
suit	connected	investment	service
system	connecting	join	serving
talked	contained	joyful	shipping
team	content	kisses	skirt
territory	corner	knew	sleet
text	crazy	knot	soap
thankful	credit	limb	steady
there	delivered	lodge	supplies
these	deserve	loyal	supply
Thursday	desired	manner	support
tiny	dirty	mister	supposed
to-night	doctor	moral	sure
towel	domestic	Mrs.	sweater
training	dwelling	musical	taking
trial	elect	national	temple
Tuesday	entertain	neighbor	their
until	establish	newspaper	themselves
upper	exact	northern	though
vision	except	noticed	throat
weary	explain	notion	through
wedding	factories	obtained	throughout
weekly	fair	ocean	title
won	famous	offered	track
worst	fancy	oh	tract
yourselves			

transportation
tread
uniform
visited
voice
waist
woman
written

94%

absolute
advising
afloat
although
artist
ashamed
assembly
assist
Ave.
avenue
badly
balance
bite
bottom
bulk
candle
can't
carefully
cashier
certain
chairman
changing
cheerful
citizen
complaint
connection
consideration
convention
cough
county
curtain
dancing
dangerous
debating
democratic
dice
difference
difficult
directed
due
extensive
fairly
fare
fault
favorable
fee
figured

foolish
fuel
garment
gentlemen
gray
grind
grove
guide
hen
higher
household
human
importance
increasing
informed
inspector
intend
interesting
junk
liberal
lie
lighting
likely
listen
lovely
maintain
model
moving
natural
no
outlined
permit
pertaining
pole
powder
preacher
priced
process
promotion
prove
publisher
quality
quite
rapidly
reception
refreshment
register
replying
rough
row
rye
satisfaction
scarce
shopping
silence
sore
spare

spirit
standard
statement
strength
studies
substitute
success
supplied
tanning
tax
term
thereof
vacation
wait
wear
winner
worthy
Xmas.

STEP 6—92%

93%

adjustment
anxious
apart
application
arrive
assured
attached
attain
attempt
attending
avoid
boarding
booth
clever
cloudy
concert
confined
consist
containing
correction
decrease
design
didn't
division
dreadful
enclosed
encourage
entirely
exam.
expired
fashion
fashionable
favored
federal
fever

finger
fitted
folk
funeral
furnace
gasoline
group
hence
holiday
honestly
humor
improving
institute
international
introduction
ironing
justified
justify
kindest
latest
liable
limit
loving
main
manager
modern
nap
neglect
nevertheless
notify
opening
organ
pa
penny
plainly
pools
prepaid
private
proceed
proved
quiet
quotation
recite
refund
regardless
reliable
requesting
scrap
seemed
server
sire
situation
skating
slide
smooth
struck
struggle

The Iowa Spelling Scales

style
subscriber
suitable
surface
taste
taught
telephone
tend
therefore
throw
tight
touch
tried
uncle
unpaid
useful
wasn't
weather
weight
whole
wholesale
whose
women
wondering
worry
you'll

92%

ability
absent
accomplish
adjusted
advancement
appointment
article
attention
author
await
break
breaking
butcher
capable
captain
chief
closely
closing
considerable
considering
constitution
cooler
crippled
delayed
delightful
detail
director
discover
disposed
dozen

eager
employed
enjoyed
enter
entitle
evidence
excess
expensive
explaining
followed
forced
forgotten
forth
fullest
government
grammar
headache
healthy
hello
hereby
housekeeping
I'd
inclined
increased
indicate
instance
instant
instructed
instructor
invitation
lbs.
linen
mental
merry
met
obligation
parent
parlor
pastor
piece
placing
policy
prepared
presume
prevail
previous
promised
quarter
quit
rabbit
recent
regard
represent
roll
route
ruin
saddle

salary
secured
seldom
seller
serious
social
submit
Thanksgiving
tickled
traveling
wage
wearing
Wednesday
workmanship

91%

adopted
affair
agriculture
ambition
applied
attraction
baking
believe
biggest
bit
blackberries
bowl
cabinet
certainly
cherries
choice
circulation
concern
creamery
creep
crew
different
drama
effort
enroll
explained
firm
ford
German
glorious
graduation
grocery
handled
handling
herein
improvement
inclose
internal
invoice
legal
loan

machinery
majority
material
mention
million
needing
neither
notified
oversight
parcel
perfectly
position
purchase
purpose
responsible
sanitary
sew
sis
stayed
to-morrow
valuable
we'll

STEP 7—88%

90%

actual
addressed
admit
arrange
blizzard
blooming
college
combination
comfortable
conclusion
confidence
considered
copies
courage
coy
cute
decided
discontinued
doubt
doubtless
either
employer
established
estimated
examined
expense
expression
favorite
fierce
following
forward

frequently
fresh
gee
grown
guest
helpful
I'm
impression
inclosed
insurance
involved
issued
item
largely
lately
liquid
loss
madam
manual
nephew
nineteen
oblige
o'clock
ordered
post office
preparing
proposition
publication
purchased
realize
recently
remembered
remembering
renewed
representation
represented
riding
rural
securing
select
selection
series
shipper
slept
slight
slightly
splendid
suggest
treasurer
university
vacant
violin
89%
accident
across
activity
agreeable

agreed
argument
arrival
arriving
banquet
billed
cedar
choose
circumstances
collar
colored
continued
dairy
deliveries
delivery
discourage
entertaining
error
exactly
fourth
freight
generous
gradually
graze
grip
happened
hesitate
independent
insert
installed
investigate
laid
mentioned
numerous
opera
ordinary
past
pattern
personality
picnic
plum
possibly
practice
profitable
queer
reasonable
satisfactory
saver
selected
shown
stating
strawberries
suggested
supervision
that's
type
volume

weigh
won't
writing
88%
ache
ankle
approval
assure
assuring
attorney
automatic
automobile
braid
Bro.
cartoon
celebrate
coming
commercial
comply
contrary
credited
current
decide
deposit
deserved
disposal
durable
earnest
engineer
exciting
exercise
fern
fortunate
forty
forwarding
friendship
further
ghost
growth
hare
headquarter
identify
impossible
inasmuch
latter
manufacture
misunderstanding
occupied
plow
prayer
procured
profit
proof
qualities
quoted
received
reference

respectfully
rifle
Saturday
sewing
sitting
society
source
studied
submitted
surplus
view
waste
weighed
87%
accordingly
announce
arranged
attach
booster
calves
canned
cellar
character
collecting
commence
conference
convince
course
data
destination
earliest
enclosing
fitting
generally
gratitude
hadn't
happiness
haste
hospital
illustrated
institution
intention
investigation
junior
knowledge
misses
namely
ought
owing
realizing
regarding
registered
remedy
remit
republican
salesman
sincere

The Iowa Spelling Scales

slippery
superior
telegram
toward
universal
urge
weren't
we've
worried
yoke
you'd

STEP 8—84%

86%

accordance
ambitious
bracelet
carrying
companies
customer
democrat
description
development
easily
effect
entry
equally
examine
exception
finally
forwarded
handkerchief
honorable
inclosing
lovingly
medicine
missed
obliged
Prof.
really
receive
reservation
resigned
straight
strict
using
usual
voting
wouldn't

85%

auditor
brief
chose
concerning
contemplating
cordial

crowded
examination
fabric
furniture
hustling
influence
journal
library
loose
neighborhood
politics
positive
premium
quote
senior
shipped
shoulder
signature
stationary
strictly
surprise
terrible
truly
utmost
whether

84%

advice
allowed
attractive
authorized
bog
capital
confident
couldn't
described
destroyed
etc.
experience
foreign
heir
illustrating
instrument
Latin
literary
meant
operation
opinion
pardon
patent
patient
possession
prosperity
satisfy
stomach
tatting
transit

83%

acknowledge
administration
advertise
association
awful
business
channel
compelled
contemplated
crocheting
desiring
enrolled
entertainment
envelope
favorably
filing
gravy
management
organize
organized
profession
raiser
refer
satisfied
secretary
stopped
studying
theater
together
too
vicinity
writer

82%

accomplished
additional
agency
altogether
annual
assortment
attitude
available
beginning
crowd
develop
difficulty
disagreeable
electrical
elsewhere
engineering
entitled
evidently
existing
figuring
handsome
hoping

illustration
manufacturing
official
operated
operating
subscription
transfer
various

STEP 9—79%

81%

acceptance
acquire
choosing
constantly
convinced
daddy
dependent
duplicate
examiner
February
graduating
individual
its
lining
lose
merchandise
particularly
science
timothy

80%

admission
associated
assume
assurance
commission
confer
congratulation
decision
enormous
enrollment
equipment
exceptional
exhibit
explanation
extreme
forenoon
genuine
hasn't
hauled
isn't
jobber
label
nervous
patron

The Iowa Spelling Scales

practical
regularly
responsibility
succeed
supervisor
79%
appreciate
assistance
ballot
bass
candidate
certificate
Christian
civics
distribution
executed
hers
inducement
legislation
magazine
maturity
maybe
principal
readily
registration
unusual
78%
advertised
appreciated
assigned
assistant
bargain
believing
clothe
confirm
control
cushion
formerly
interfere
pleasant
relieve
resource
surprised
talent
worrying
77%
actually
consequently
correspond
coupon
crochet
demonstrated
demonstration
disgusted
haven't
imagine

mamma
ninety
organization
prosperous
successful
sympathy

STEP 10—73%
76%
applicant
electricity
excitement
familiar
heretofore
immediate
merely
orchestra
physical
planned
preparation
presence
receiving
relieved
requirement
similar
variety
vary
75%
advisable
algebra
associate
awfully
carnival
co-operation
disease
Dr.
employee
mere
naturally
necessity
sense
Tues.
welfare
74%
advertising
alfalfa
appreciating
basis
benefit
campaign
catalogue
congratulate
consequence
conservatory
especially

excellent
exclusively
merit
necessary
quantity
reliability
response
separate
73%
aren't
choir
commissioner
committee
co-operative
extension
inquiry
meter
ninth
possibility
practicing
renewal
safety
straightened
succeeded
72%
agricultural
alley
appearance
capacity
community
confirming
corporation
notary
usually
71%
administrator
amendment
attendance
coarse
compliment
cordially
customary
installment
niece
soliciting
surgery
70%
advertisement
appreciation
arrangement
assignment
based
bureau
considerably
convenience

exhibition
hastily
original
preliminary
specification

STEP 11—66%
69%
acquainted
correspondent
disappointed
epidemic
inferior
license
sincerely
specially
68%
athletics
doesn't
exceptionally
mechanical
occasion
passed
probably
67%
allotment
announcement
authority
bonus
definite
efficient
essential
exhausted
librarian
nickel
personally
planning
professional
regretting
remittance
sufficient
66%
absolutely
consultation
ere
good-bye
quantities
receipt
unnecessary
65%
barely
communication
completely
executive

extremely
financial
inquiries
literature
representative

64%
calendar
leisure
opportunity
solicit

63%
annually
practically
semester
superintendent

STEP 12—58%

62%
client
convenient
council
immense
permanent
principle

61%
accredited
characteristic
courteous
losing
scientific

60%
analysis
correspondence
mortgage
Sabbath

59%
enthusiastic
lieutenant
unusually

58%
all right
alumni
anticipate
assessment
candidacy
continuous
fundamental
geometry
girlie
physician
possess
thorough

57%
thoroughly

56%
accompanying
acquaintance
auntie
originally
recommendation

55%
anticipating
circuit
disappoint
equipped
immediately

STEP 13—50%

54%
confirmation
materially
recommend
thesis

53%
pneumonia
referred

52%
satisfactorily

51%
bulletin
disappointment
grateful
referring

50%
apparatus
co-operating
inconvenience
judgment
rec'd

49%
efficiency
inst.
remembrance

48%
grippe
prior

47%
affectionately

46%
politician
tuberculosis

STEP 14—42%

45%
affidavit

44%
ingredients
privilege

43%
guarantee
rheumatism

42%
appendicitis
Hallowe'en

41%
conveniently
enthusiasm
guaranteed
occasionally

39%
accommodate
peculiarities

38%
schedule

STEP 15—34%

37%
definitely
fraternally

35%
anniversary

34%
zephyr

33%
chautauqua
X-ray

31%
canvass

STEP 16—27%

28%
phosphorus

APPENDIX

EXHIBIT A

Set I, list 1 illustrates the form in which words were sent to the various schools.

Iowa Spelling List—1-1

1	and	26	recently	51	fraternally	76	attractive
2	me	27	pupil	52	broke	77	management
3	some	28	correct	53	cake	78	toy
4	think	29	walk	54	blood	79	singing
5	say	30	Dr.	55	renewal	80	forenoon
6	each	31	happen	56	confident	81	durable
7	way	32	top	57	colored	82	per cent
8	great	33	window	58	roll	83	kitten
9	put	34	shipping	59	clock	84	plow
10	picture	35	wife	60	forced	85	faster
11	market	36	standard	61	outfit	86	breaking
12	folk	37	printed	62	thorough	87	brand
13	real	38	fifty	63	waste	88	soap
14	sorry	39	cream	64	grown	89	calendar
15	leave	40	recommend	65	stick	90	anniversary
16	aunt	41	prior	66	deep	91	extreme
17	credit	42	crowd	67	organized	92	possess
18	supply	43	forwarded	68	exceptional	93	kinder
19	street	44	cool	69	weigh	94	slept
20	profit	45	rush	70	applicant	95	dice
21	begin	46	represented	71	porch	96	federal
22	net	47	publication	72	staying	·97	insert
23	May	48	blow	73	instructed	98	likewise
24	brought	49	fixed.	74	slightly	99	identify
25	Oct.	50	newspaper	75	tie	100	daddy

EXHIBIT B

Instructions sent with spelling material to all cooperating teachers.

INSTRUCTIONS TO TEACHERS

This work is a part of a state wide effort to grade a list of most commonly used words. The success of the work will depend upon the accuracy with which you and all other teachers follow these directions.

Please have your pupils spell one list each day; 100 words if you are teaching grades V to VIII and 50 words if you are teaching grades II, III or IV. Pronounce each word distinctly and make sure that each child understands the word. Give a short illustrative sentence in all cases where different words have the same or similar pronunciation. The words are to be given without previous study or drill of any kind. Give plenty of time but no assistance.

Have the work done with pencil, on paper of uniform size, writing two columns on a page but do **not** write on both sides of the paper. The child should write his name, sex, age, and grade and the name of his school and city at the top of each sheet. Pronounce the words in order numbered and have the pupils number the words as they write them. This is very important.

Impress upon the children that in case of an error, they are to draw a line through the word and write it correctly above or beside the misspelled word. Words in which one letter has been written over another will be counted wrong, as it is almost impossible to know which was the child's final decision on the spelling.

It is recognized that in the lower grades many of these words are quite unfamiliar to the children and that a large proportion of the pupils will not be able to spell most of the words in the list. The only way, however, to find out what words the children can spell and what words they cannot spell is to give them the opportunity to attempt to spell all the words. Keep them just as happy in the effort as possible by telling them that other boys and girls of the same grade are trying to spell the same words in other schools in Iowa. If you are teaching in grade II or III, it will probably be better to pronounce 25 words in the forenoon and 25 in the afternoon than to give all 50 at once.

If your pupils are in grades VI, VII, or VIII, will you please assist in the scoring by having a few of the stronger pupils detailed each day to check the papers of all members of the class. Caution them that they are not to mark the word in any way but only make a cross through the number of the word which is misspelled. Four children can correct the papers for a room in twenty to thirty minutes and you will doubtless have no difficulty in finding some of the pupils who will very gladly do this.

The papers are to be collected each day and tied together. At the end of the ten days, the ten bunches of papers which represent the ten days' spelling of the pupils in your room, are to be sent tied in a single package to your superintendent. He will then forward these papers with all others from your city to the Extension Division. The Extension Division will score the papers from the lower grades and tabulate the spellings from all contributing schools and return the results to your Superintendent.

To the extent that these instructions are carefully followed and your cooperation secured will the results be of value to all the schools of the state. Please give the work your best effort but do not attempt to improve the spelling of the children of your room on these words by assisting them in their spelling in any way.

EXHIBIT C

Cities Co-operating in Spelling Study

Adair	Denison	Lake View	Oskaloosa
Algona	Dunlap	Lansing	Ottumwa
Ames	Eddyville	La Porte City	Pella
Belle Plaine	Eldon	Le Mars	Pocahontas
Belmond	Fairfield	Lineville	Postville
Bloomfield	Glenwood	Manilla	Red Oak
Bonaparte	Grinnell	Manson	Reinbeck
Boone	Griswold	Marengo	Remsen
Britt	Guttenburg	Marshalltown	Rockford
Buffalo Center	Hampton	Montezuma	Rockwell City
Burlington	Hartley	Monticello	Rolfe
Carroll	Hawarden	Moulton	Sheldon
Casey	Hopkinton	Muscatine	Sidney
Centerville	Humboldt	Nashua	Sigourney
Chariton	Humeston	Nevada	Sioux Center
Charles City	Ida Grove	New Hampton	Spirit Lake
Cherokee	Independence	New London	State Center
Clarinda	Inwood	New Sharon	Stuart
Clarion	Iowa City	Newton	Toledo
Clinton	Jewell	Northwood	Waterloo, E.
Corning	Keokuk	Oakland	Waukon
Corydon	Keosauqua	Oelwein	What Cheer
Council Bluffs	Kingsley	Orange City	Williamsburg
Cresco	Knoxville	Osage	Woodbine
Davenport	Lake Mills		

OK IS DUE ON THE LAST
STAMPED BELOW

AN INITIAL FINE OF 25 C
WILL BE ASSESSED FOR FAILURE TO R
THIS BOOK ON THE DATE DUE. THE
WILL INCREASE TO
DAY AND TO $1.0
OVERDUE.

1932

10Jul'57MH

MAY 21

NOV 21 1945

APR 22 1

17

LD 2

CPSIA information can be obtained
at www.ICGtesting.com
Printed in the USA
FSOW03n2029150916
25080FS